Excel

ADVANCED SKILLS

ENGLISH

YEAR 2

AGES 7–8

ADVANCED ENGLISH

Get the Results You Want!

PASCAL PRESS

Tanya Dalgleish

Contents

Introduction

The aim of the ***Excel*** **Advanced Skills: Advanced English** series is to build on and extend students' skills in English. Each book in the series supports the requirements of the Australian Curriculum (English) at each year level.

The series consists of six books, one for each year level, from Year 1 to Year 6. The series is supported by other books in the ***Excel*** **Advanced Skills English** range.

Structure of the book

Each book in the series contains:

- thirty carefully graded, three-page units of teaching and learning activities.
  - Unit A includes a sample informative, imaginative or persuasive text and deals with **Reading and comprehension skills**.
  - Unit B deals with the Conventions of language: **Spelling**, **Vocabulary**, **Grammar** and **Punctuation**.
  - Unit C deals with **Texts in context**. It provides for a deeper analysis and evaluation of the language choices authors make and the ways that readers make meaning from texts.
- four double-page NAPLAN-style tests.
- answers for all questions.

How to use this book

- Students should complete one unit per week. A suggested plan would be to complete the week's Unit A and B page on one day and the Unit C page on another day of the same week.
- After successfully completing a set of units (e.g. 1–7, 8–15, 16–23, 24–30), students should undertake the corresponding NAPLAN-style test.

How to use this book with the *Excel* Advanced Skills: Advanced Mathematics series

For a complete **weekly English and Mathematics program**, use this book in conjunction with the ***Excel*** **Advanced Skills: Advanced Mathematics Year 2** book. This way a student will have work set for four days a week: two days for English and two days for Mathematics.

Excel ADVANCED SKILLS MATHS YEAR 2 AGES 7–8 ADVANCED MATHEMATICS Get the Results You Want! Tanya Dalgleish

How to assess students' progress

- Templates are included in each book of the series that outline the knowledge and skills targeted by the questions in that book. (Please see page 6.)
- The questions move through the subtopics of English in exactly the same order in each book but as there are more questions and more complex material included in later years of the Year 1 to Year 6 continuum, the question numbers vary across the books.
- The results of the work undertaken in Units A and B can be recorded on the marking grid. See ways to use the marking grid on page 4.

Excel Advanced Skills titles

If students are having difficulty in any area, further support is available in other ***Excel*** workbooks. Please see the comprehensive list on page 5.

The *Excel* step-by-step improvement plan

Step 1

Read the introduction on page 3.

Step 2

Read the text below, along with the further explanation about the question templates and marking grids on pages 6 and 7.

Question templates

These outline the knowledge and skills targeted by the questions in the book. Remember that the questions move through the subtopics of English in exactly the same order.

Marking grids

The results of the work undertaken in Units A and B can be recorded on the marking grid. This is an easy-to-use diagnostic tool that indicates each student's strengths and weaknesses in relation to specific areas of English.

These results can be used to gather extra information about each student's progress and revision needs. For example, see the sample marking grid for reading and comprehension in the right-hand column:

- When marking answers on the grid, simply mark incorrect answers with 'X' in the appropriate box. This will result in a graphical representation of areas needing further work. An example for the first five units is shown above. If a question has several parts, it should be counted wrong if one or more mistakes are made.
- Remember that you can identify exactly what type of questions a student is having difficulty with in a topic. For example, in the grid above the student is having difficulty with reading and comprehension evaluative questions.
- There is no marking grid for Unit C.

Marking grid

Reading and comprehension	Literal	Literal	Inferring	Inferring	Inferring	Evaluative
Question	**1**	**2**	**3**	**4**	**5**	**6**
Unit 1						
Unit 2						X
Unit 3						
Unit 4						X
Unit 5						X
Unit 6						
Unit 7						
Unit 8						
Unit 9						
Unit 10						

This grid indicates that the student needs extra help and practice in evaluative questions.

Step 3

Refer to page 5: ***Excel* books to help you *get the results you want*!**

- Under each topic there is a list of books in our range to help students. Each ***Excel*** book has a comprehensive contents page that will help you find the appropriate pages in the book to target the specific topic you want in each subject area.

Excel books to help you *get the results you want!*

Reading and comprehension

Excel Advanced Skills

9781741255690

Excel NAPLAN*-style Tests

9781741254518

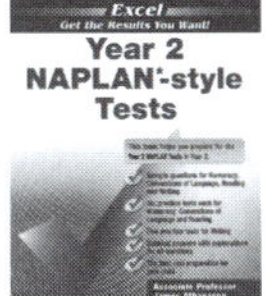

9781741254099

Spelling

Excel Advanced Skills

9781741254655

Excel NAPLAN*-style Tests

9781741254518

9781741254099

Excel Handbooks & Guides

9781864410617

Vocabulary

Excel Advanced Skills

9781741254655

Excel NAPLAN*-style Tests

9781741254518

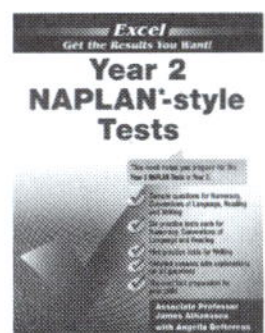

9781741254099

Grammar

Excel Advanced Skills

9781741254426

Excel NAPLAN*-style Tests

9781741254518

9781741254099

Excel Handbooks & Guides

9781864410600

Punctuation

Excel Advanced Skills

9781741254426

Excel NAPLAN*-style Tests

9781741254518

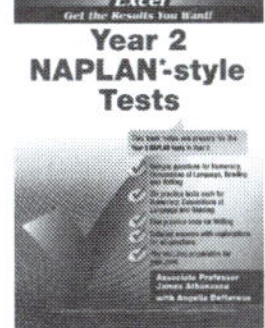

9781741254099

Writing

Excel Advanced Skills

9781741254402

Excel NAPLAN*-style Tests

9781741254518

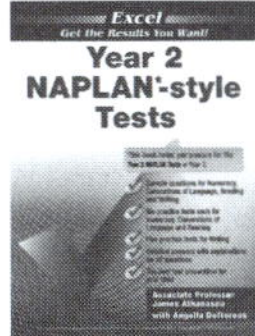

9781741254099

Question templates

Reading and comprehension

Q1–2 Literal: Answers to these questions are found directly in the text.

Q3–5 Inferring: Answers to these questions need to be worked out from clues in the text.

Q6 Evaluative: Answers to this question rely on making judgements about information in the text and beyond the text.

Spelling

Q1–4 Misspelt words: In these questions, students use their understanding of spelling patterns and rules to correct the mistakes.

Q5 Word families: In this question, students use their knowledge of word roots, prefixes and suffixes to build word groups.

Vocabulary

Q6 Synonyms: In this question, students need to recognise similarities of meanings

Q7 Meanings in context/ Word usage: In this question students need to comprehend the meanings and usage of words in context.

Q8 Definitions: In this question students are required to demonstrate understanding of word meanings and usage in the context of the text.

Q9 Antonyms: In this question, students need to understand similarities and differences of word meanings

Grammar

Q10 Nouns/Noun groups/ Tense: This question deals with aspects of nouns and noun groups, e.g. common nouns, proper nouns, adjectives and articles.

Q11 Verbs/Verb groups: This question deals with aspects of verbs and verb groups, e.g. action (doing), thinking or sensing verbs; saying, relating (being), auxiliary (helping) verbs and tense.

Q12 Adverbials/Conjunctions/ Pronouns: This question deals with adverbials: words or phrases that tell when, where and how.

Q13 Cohesion: This question deals with different types of sentences using conjunctions (and, but, so, because, although, since, until) and noun–pronoun reference.

Punctuation

Q14–15 These questions deal with ways of punctuating sentences, e.g. adding capital letters, full stops, question marks, exclamation marks, commas, quotation marks and apostrophes.

Texts in context

Note: There is no marking grid for Unit C questions.

Q1–6 These questions deal with aspects of text, including:

Purpose and audience: These questions require students to recognise the purpose of a text (such as to inform, persuade or entertain) and the nature of its intended audience (the reader, listener or viewer).

Text structures and features: These questions require students to examine the ways a text is organised through, for example, sequencing, paragraphing and cohesive devices.

Textual interpretations: These questions require students to analyse the text and its effectiveness through, for example, language choices, imagery and point of view.

Get creative

Q7 This task requires students to create their own texts by adding to or responding to the models provided. Student responses will vary as this task is open-ended.

This icon indicates where students will need to use their own paper to answer the question.

Marking grid

Reading and comprehension	Literal	Literal	Inferring	Inferring	Inferring	Evaluative
Question	1	2	3	4	5	6
Unit 1						
Unit 2						
Unit 3						
Unit 4						
Unit 5						
Unit 6						
Unit 7						
Unit 8						
Unit 9						
Unit 10						
Unit 11						
Unit 12						
Unit 13						
Unit 14						
Unit 15						
Unit 16						
Unit 17						
Unit 18						
Unit 19						
Unit 20						
Unit 21						
Unit 22						
Unit 23						
Unit 24						
Unit 25						
Unit 26						
Unit 27						
Unit 28						
Unit 29						
Unit 30						
Question	1	2	3	4	5	6

Marking grid

Conventions of language	Spelling					Vocabulary				Grammar				Punctuation	
	Misspelt words	Misspelt words	Misspelt words	Misspelt words	Word families	Synonyms	Meanings in context/ Word usage	Definitions	Antonyms	Nouns/ Noun groups	Verbs/Verb groups/ Tense	Adverbials/ Conjunctions/ Pronouns	Cohesion	Punctuation	Punctuation
Question	1	2	3	4	5	6	7	8	9	10	11	12	13	14	15
Unit 1															
Unit 2															
Unit 3															
Unit 4															
Unit 5															
Unit 6															
Unit 7															
Unit 8															
Unit 9															
Unit 10															
Unit 11															
Unit 12															
Unit 13															
Unit 14															
Unit 15															
Unit 16															
Unit 17															
Unit 18															
Unit 19															
Unit 20															
Unit 21															
Unit 22															
Unit 23															
Unit 24															
Unit 25															
Unit 26															
Unit 27															
Unit 28															
Unit 29															
Unit 30															
Question	1	2	3	4	5	6	7	8	9	10	11	12	13	14	15

Joshua's jam

I made jam for Mum's birthday. This is what I did.

Firstly I thawed some frozen raspberries and blueberries. Then I mixed them in sugar and lemon juice. Then I heated the mixture in a saucepan on the stove. I kept stirring while it cooked.

When the berries were dissolved and the mixture looked like jam, I turned off the stove and left the jam to cool.

Once it had cooled I poured the jam into really clean jars with screw-top lids.

I put some jam and cream on the scones and took them to Mum. (The scones came from the bakery.)

Mum loved my jam.

By Josh

1. Why did Josh make jam?
   - **A** because he had a recipe
   - **B** because he likes jam
   - **C** for Mum's birthday
2. What kind of jam did Josh make?
   - **A** raspberry jam
   - **B** berry jam
   - **C** blueberry jam
3. Where did the scones come from?
   - **A** Josh made them.
   - **B** Josh bought them in a shop.
   - **C** Mum gave them to Josh.
4. Choose **all** that apply. Which ingredients are needed to make the jam?
   - **A** raspberries
   - **B** blueberries
   - **C** a saucepan
   - **D** a stove
   - **E** sugar
   - **F** lemon juice
5. Josh keeps the jam
   - **A** in jars.
   - **B** in a saucepan.
   - **C** on the stove.
6. How did Mum feel about the jam?

....

....

Answers and explanations on page 106

SPELLING

Write the correct spelling of the underlined words in questions 1–4.

1 It was Mum's berthday.

....

2 Mix in the suger.

....

3 Poor the jam into a jar.

....

4 The sausepan was on the stove.

....

5 Write three words from the word family that includes **mixed**.

....

....

....

VOCABULARY

6 Circle the answer that has the nearest meaning to the underlined word.

Josh kept stirring the jam.

A simmering **B** mangling
C mixing **D** cooking

7 Write a word from the text to match the meaning.

when something solid has turned into liquid

....

8 Add a word from the text to complete the sentence.

The jars were really ....

9 Circle the word that does **not** belong.

A put **B** removed
C placed **D** deposited

GRAMMAR

10 Complete the sentence with a common noun from the text.

We ate .... with jam and cream.

11 Choose the correct action (doing) verb to complete the sentence.

Firstly I .... some frozen berries.

A thaw
B thaws
C thawed
D thawing

12 Write a prepositional phrase from the text that tells **where**.

I poured the jam ....

....

13 Choose a pronoun to correctly complete the sentence.

I put some jam and cream on the scones and took .... to Mum.

A they
B it
C her
D them

PUNCTUATION

Rewrite the sentences correctly.

14 I made jam for mum

....

....

15 who likes scones

....

....

Answers and explanations on page 106

Joshua's jam

I made jam for Mum's birthday. This is what I did.

Firstly I thawed some frozen raspberries and blueberries. Then I mixed them in sugar and lemon juice. Then I heated the mixture in a saucepan on the stove. I kept stirring while it cooked.

When the berries were dissolved and the mixture looked like jam, I turned off the stove and left the jam to cool.

Once it had cooled I poured the jam into really clean jars with screw-top lids.

I put some jam and cream on the scones and took them to Mum. (The scones came from the bakery.)

Mum loved my jam.

By Josh

1 The text
- A is a recipe for jam.
- B tells what Josh did.
- C describes scones and jam.

2 Could you use the text to make Josh's jam?
- A No, because it doesn't say how long it takes to cook.
- B Yes, because it tells you which ingredients to use.
- C No, because it doesn't tell you how much of each ingredient to use.

3 What is the structure of the text?
- A list of ingredients, method
- B orientation, complication, resolution
- C introduction, sequence of events, conclusion

4 The following words help sequence events in time. Find and circle them in the text.

Firstly	Then	Then	When	Once

5 Another title for the text could be
- A How to cook jam.
- B Mum's birthday treat.
- C Josh's scones.

6 Choose **all** that apply. Josh decided to cook jam because
- A he knew how.
- B his mum likes jam on scones.
- C his mum trusts him in the kitchen.

7 Make a poster that lists safety rules for working in the kitchen. Plan your poster here.

Answers and explanations on page 106

All about me

Write your answers on the lines to fill in the form.

Name	Mia Edwards
Age	7
Address	4/41 Banksia St, Drummoyne, NSW 2047
Who I live with	Mum and Harper
My friend(s)	Ethan and Tomoko
My favourite colour	blue
My favourite food	mangoes
My favourite hobbies and interests	swimming, playing in the park, dancing
My favourite subject at school	Maths
If I could be an animal I would be	a dolphin
Why?	because they swim all day and they like to play and they love each other
When I grow up I want to	help animals
Describe where you live	I live in a unit. It has two bedrooms. I share a bedroom with Harper. we have bunk beds. She sleeps on the top bunk because she is older than me. When Harper has a sleepover at a friend's place, Mum lets me sleep on Harper's bunk.

My home

1 Choose **all** that apply. Who lives with Mia?

- **A** Ethan
- **B** Tomoko
- **C** Mum
- **D** Dad
- **E** Harper

2 How many bedrooms are there in Mia's home?

- **A** one
- **B** two
- **C** three

3 Mia would prefer

- **A** her own bedroom.
- **B** the top bunk.
- **C** the bottom bunk.

4 Mia is likely to be

- **A** a poor swimmer.
- **B** an average swimmer.
- **C** a good swimmer.

5 Mia thinks dolphins

- **A** have a good life.
- **B** have a difficult life.
- **C** are beautiful.

6 What does Mia value most?

....

....

Answers and explanations on page 106

SPELLING

Write the correct spelling of the underlined words in questions 1–4.

1 Her favourite color is blue.

2 Mia loves swiming.

3 Ethan is a frend.

4 Mia shares a bedrewm with her sister.

5 Write three words from the word family that includes **sleep**.

VOCABULARY

6 Circle the answer that has the nearest meaning to the underlined word.

Mia wants to help animals.

A support B love
C feed D shelter

7 Write a word from the text to match the meaning.

something that you enjoy doing on a regular basis

8 Add a word from the text to complete the sentence.

Maths is Mia's favourite .... at school.

9 Circle the word that does **not** belong.

A mango B apple
C banana D cheese

GRAMMAR

10 Complete the sentence with a common noun from the text.

A .... is a sea animal.

11 Choose the correct action (doing) verb to complete the sentence.

Harper sometimes .... at her friend's place.

A sleep
B is sleeping
C are sleeping
D sleeps

12 Write a prepositional phrase from the text that tells **where**.

Mia sometimes sleeps ....

13 Choose a pronoun to correctly complete the sentence.

Harper and I share a bedroom.

.... have bunk beds.

A They B It
C We D She

PUNCTUATION

Rewrite the sentences correctly.

14 sometimes harper has a sleepover

15 mia lives in drummoyne

Answers and explanations on page 106

TEXTS IN CONTEXT

All about me

Write your answers on the lines to fill in the form.

Name	Mia Edwards
Age	7
Address	4/41 Banksia St, Drummoyne, NSW 2047
Who I live with	Mum and Harper
My friend(s)	Ethan and Tomoko
My favourite colour	blue
My favourite food	mangoes
My favourite hobbies and interests	swimming, playing in the park, dancing
My favourite subject at school	Maths
If I could be an animal I would be	a dolphin
Why?	because they swim all day and they like to play and they love each other
When I grow up I want to	help animals
Describe where you live	I live in a unit. It has two bedrooms. I share a bedroom with Harper. We have bunk beds. She sleeps on the top bunk because she is older than me. When Harper has a sleepover at a friend's place, Mum lets me sleep on Harper's bunk.

My home

1 Why might Mia have filled in this form?
- A so she can get to know herself
- B so people who don't know her can find out about her
- C to tell her best friends about herself

2 Choose **two** answers. Who might find Mia's answers useful?
- A her mum
- B Ethan and Tomoko
- C children in her class
- D her teacher

3 Mia's answers in the text are
- A made up.
- B exaggerated.
- C wrong.
- D factual.

4 The photograph shows
- A Mia's unit block.
- B Mia's school.
- C Where Mia's mother works.

5 Is Mia someone you might like as a friend? Explain.

....

....

6 If you were Harper, how would you feel about Mia sleeping in your bed? Explain.

....

....

....

7 Write your own answers to the questions on the form.

Answers and explanations on pages 106–107

Be quiet, Scoobie!

Our neighbour's dog was barking again.

'Scoobie, shush!' I called across from our balcony to Scoobie.

'He's just bored, Liam,' said Dad.

'He'll get into trouble. Mr Timble upstairs will report him to the Council again. Can we offer to help, Dad? Otherwise Jackie might have to give Scoobie away.'

'Mmm … maybe. It isn't fair for him to be locked up in that unit all day, alone, while Jackie's at work. That's not much of a life. He's bored and lonely. No wonder he barks. I'll talk to Jackie.'

'Jackie will let us take Scoobie to the park in the afternoon, Dad. I know she will. And Scoobie will be so happy.'

'Looking after a dog is a big responsibility but I will talk to Jackie,' replied Dad.

1 What is the dog doing?
A running   B barking   C growling

2 The dog lives .... Liam.
A above   B below   C across from

3 Who's locked up all day?
A Mr Timble   B Jackie   C Scoobie

4 Why is the dog unhappy? Choose **all** that apply.
A Jackie is at work.
B Mr Timble is yelling at him.
C He is bored and lonely.

5 What does Liam think will make the dog happy?
A going to the park   B telling it to shush   C living with Liam

6 Who is Dad most concerned about?

....

....

Answers and explanations on page 107

SPELLING

Write the correct spelling of the underlined words in questions 1–4.

1 Mr Timble lives upstares.

....

2 Liam called acros to Scoobie.

....

3 It isn't fare to lock Scoobie up all day.

....

4 Take Scoobie to the park in the aftarnoon.

....

5 Write three words from the word family that includes **bored**.

....

....

....

VOCABULARY

6 Circle the answer that has the nearest meaning to the underlined word.

Scoobie stood on the balcony.

A unit
B tiles
C verandah
D ledge

7 Write a word from the text to match the meaning.

a duty to do something properly

....

8 Add a word from the text to complete the sentence.

Barking dogs can be reported to the

....

9 Circle the word that does **not** belong.

A cheerful
B deserted
C lonely
D abandoned

GRAMMAR

10 Complete the sentence with a common noun from the text.

Jackie is Liam's ....

11 Choose the correct action (doing) verb to complete the sentence.

Liam wants to ....
Scoobie to the park.

A taking
B taken
C took
D take

12 Write a prepositional phrase from the text that tells **where**.

Scoobie is locked ....

.... all day.

13 Choose a pronoun to correctly complete the sentence.

Scoobie is barking. ....
is bored.

A He
B She
C We
D Him

PUNCTUATION

Rewrite the sentences correctly.

14 be quiet

....

....

15 can we help

....

....

Answers and explanations on page 107

Be quiet, Scoobie!

Our neighbour's dog was barking again.

'Scoobie, shush!' I called across from our balcony to Scoobie.

'He's just bored, Liam,' said Dad.

'He'll get into trouble. Mr Timble upstairs will report him to the Council again. Can we offer to help, Dad? Otherwise Jackie might have to give Scoobie away.'

'Mmm … maybe. It isn't fair for him to be locked up in that unit all day, alone, while Jackie's at work. That's not much of a life. He's bored and lonely. No wonder he barks. I'll talk to Jackie.'

'Jackie will let us take Scoobie to the park in the afternoon, Dad. I know she will. And Scoobie will be so happy.'

'Looking after a dog is a big responsibility but I will talk to Jackie,' replied Dad.

1 The text
- **A** tells about Dad and the family.
- **B** records a conversation.
- **C** recounts events that happened.

2 The photograph
- **A** supports the text.
- **B** adds extra information to the text.
- **C** does not match the text.

3 Choose **all** that apply. The text includes
- **A** speech marks.
- **B** technical terms.
- **C** saying verbs.
- **D** points of view.

4 The text presents a problem and a possible solution. Write them on the lines. Then suggest an extra solution of your own.

Problem: ....

....

Possible solution: ....

....

Extra solution: ....

....

5 What does Liam expect Jackie to say?
- **A** No, it's too big a responsibility.
- **B** Yes, Scoobie would love that.
- **C** You'll need to check with your dad.
- **D** No, I'd worry about Scoobie's safety.

6 Complete the sentences.

Mr Timble should report Scoobie to the Council because ....

Mr Timble should not report Scoobie to the Council because ....

7 Imagine you are the dog on the balcony. What are you thinking or sensing?

Answers and explanations on page 107

The Bad Child's Book of Beasts

Author: Hilaire Belloc; Illustrator: BTB (Basil Temple Blackwood); Published 1896

The Elephant

When people call this beast to mind,
They marvel more and more
At such a *little* tail behind,

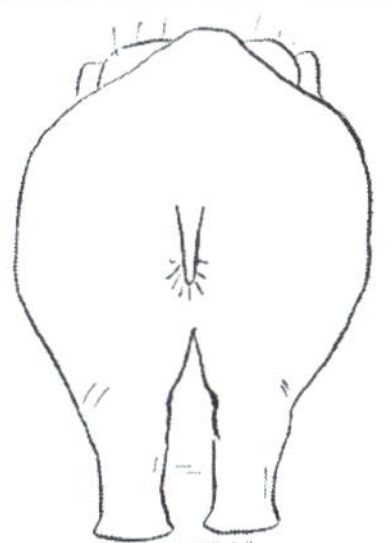

So *LARGE* a trunk before.

The Dodo

The Dodo used to walk around,
And take the sun and air.
The sun yet warms his native ground—
The Dodo is not there!
The voice which used to squawk and squeak
Is now for ever dumb—
Yet may you see his bones and beak
All in the Mu-se-um.

Source: The Project Gutenberg Ebook at www.gutenberg.net

1 The poems were published in ....

2 The poet's name is ....

3 The poet says people 'marvel' at
- **A** the size of the elephant's tail.
- **B** how odd it looks to have a larger trunk than tail.
- **C** how odd the elephant's trunk looks.

4 Choose **two** answers. In the museum, you **cannot** see the Dodo's
- **A** bones.
- **B** beak.
- **C** skin.
- **D** feathers.

5 The dodo does not 'walk around' anymore because it
- **A** is in a museum.
- **B** is extinct.
- **C** has been caught.

6 What do you think of the illustrations? ....

....

Answers and explanations on page 107

SPELLING

Write the correct spelling of the underlined words in questions 1–4.

1 An elephant is a beest.

2 The elephant's trunk is larje.

3 Dodo's could sqwork.

4 The Dodo is forever dum.

5 Write three words from the word family that includes **marvel**.

VOCABULARY

6 Circle the answer that has the nearest meaning to the underlined word.

The sun yet warms his native ground.

A soil B museum
C natural D wilderness

7 Write a word from the text to match the meaning.

a building displaying objects that are old, important or interesting

8 Add a word from the text to complete the sentence.

An elephant's nose is called a ______.

9 Circle the word that does **not** belong.

A marvel B wonder
C disregard D admire

GRAMMAR

10 Complete the sentence with a common noun from the text.

Another word for elephant, in the poem, is ______.

11 Choose the correct action (doing) verb to complete the sentence.

The dodo used to ______ around.

A walking
B walked
C walks
D walk

12 Write a prepositional phrase from the text that tell **where**.

The place to see a dodo is ______.

13 Choose a pronoun to correctly complete the sentence.

People marvel at the elephant.

______ marvel at its size.

A It B They
C We D Us

PUNCTUATION

Rewrite the sentences correctly.

14 why did it disappear

15 look there

Answers and explanations on page 107

The Bad Child's Book of Beasts

Author: Hilaire Belloc; Illustrator: BTB (Basil Temple Blackwood); Published 1896

The Elephant

When people call this beast to mind,
They marvel more and more
At such a *little* tail behind,

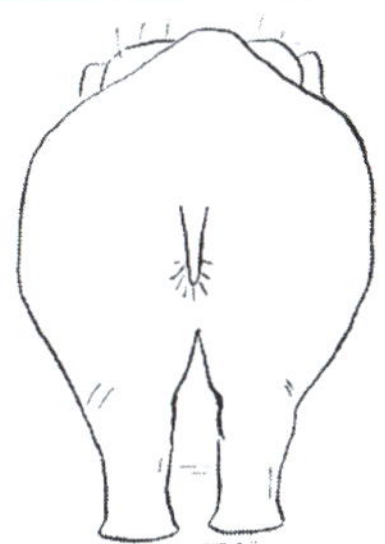

So *LARGE* a trunk before.

The Dodo

The Dodo used to walk around,
And take the sun and air.
The sun yet warms his native ground—
The Dodo is not there!
The voice which used to squawk and squeak
Is now for ever dumb—
Yet may you see his bones and beak
All in the Mu-se-um.

Source: The Project Gutenberg Ebook at www.gutenberg.net

1 What is the purpose of the poems?
- **A** to teach children to read
- **B** to describe the features of beasts
- **C** to entertain by pointing out the features of animals

2 Why would a poet call his book of poems *The Bad Child's Book of Beasts*?
- **A** Bad children like these kinds of poems.
- **B** The title is likely to make all children want to read the book.
- **C** It's a book for bad children only.

3 Find and write examples of the devices used by the poet.

changing font and letter size:

....

alliteration:

....

4 Circle the rhyming words in each poem.

5 In the first poem, 'call this beast to mind' (line 4) means
- **A** think about it.
- **B** look at the picture.
- **C** talk to each other about it.

6 In the second poem, 'dumb' (line 14) means
- **A** stupid.
- **B** silent.
- **C** always squawking and squeaking.

7 Choose an animal that has unusual features. Write a poem about it. Try to use rhyme and alliteration. Illustrate your poem.

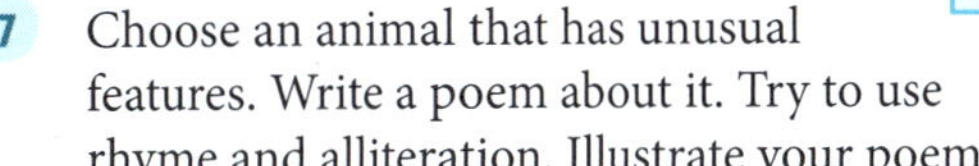

Answers and explanations on page 107

READING AND COMPREHENSION

Concert

BEST MUSIC EVENT IN ROZELLE!

Entry by gold coin donation. We are raising money for UNICEF to help children in need.

4–6 pm Saturday 10 April 10 Beatie St, Rozelle Come and see our great band **à l'improviste** (out of the blue) featuring Rianne, Ellie, Lexi and Skyla

Bring picnic rugs and portable chairs. BYO drinks and snacks.

For more information contact 4outoftheblue@mail.com

Lexi: That's me in the middle at the front. We named our band **à l'improviste.** This is a French term for 'out of the blue'. My mum was born in France and when I told her I was forming a band she said that it was unexpected.

1. When will the concert be held?

   ....

   ....

2. What does the band's name mean?

   ....

   ....

   ....

3. Money raised at the concert
   - **A** can be spent by the band.
   - **B** covers the band's costs.
   - **C** will be donated to charity.

4. The main singer for the band is
   - **A** Rianne.
   - **B** Ellie.
   - **C** Lexi.
   - **D** Skyla.

5. When Lexi's mum first heard about the band she was
   - **A** pleased.
   - **B** surprised.
   - **C** annoyed.

6. Do you think the band members are confident or shy? Are they good organisers?

   ....

   ....

   ....

   ....

   ....

   ....

Answers and explanations on page 108

SPELLING

Write the correct spelling of the underlined words in questions 1–4.

1 Entree is by donation.

....

2 The band is raising muney.

....

3 Bring portible chairs.

....

4 It is a musik event.

....

5 Write three words from the word family that includes **unexpected**.

....

....

....

VOCABULARY

6 Circle the answer that has the nearest meaning to the underlined word.

Please give a donation.

A deposit	B gold coin
C contribution	D payment

7 Write a word from the text to match the meaning.

United Nations Children's Fund

....

8 Write the word from the text that means **something that can be easily carried**.

....

9 Circle the word that does **not** belong.

A show	B parade
C concert	D performance

GRAMMAR

10 Complete the sentence with a common noun from the text.

The girls are putting on a

....

11 Choose the correct relating (being) verb to complete the sentence.

The band .... raising funds for UNICEF.

A are
B is
C have
D has

12 Write a prepositional phrase from the text that tells **where**.

Lexi's mum was born ....

....

13 Choose a pronoun to correctly complete the sentence.

The girls are performing on Saturday. I am going to see ....

A us	B they
C we	D them

PUNCTUATION

Rewrite the sentences correctly.

14 the concert is at 10 beatie st

....

....

....

15 are you going on saturday

....

....

Answers and explanations on page 108

Concert

BEST MUSIC EVENT IN ROZELLE!

Entry by gold coin donation.
We are raising money for UNICEF
to help children in need.

4–6 pm Saturday 10 April
10 Beatie St, Rozelle
Come and see our great band
à l'improviste (out of the blue)
featuring Rianne, Ellie, Lexi and Skyla

Bring picnic rugs and portable chairs.
BYO drinks and snacks.

For more information contact
4outoftheblue@mail.com

Lexi: That's me in the middle at the front. We named our band **à l'improviste.** This is a French term for 'out of the blue'. My mum was born in France and when I told her I was forming a band she said that it was unexpected.

1 The purpose of the text is to
- **A** persuade people to come to a concert.
- **B** inform people about a band.
- **C** entertain people with music.

2 Choose **all** that apply. The audience for the text is likely
- **A** the children's friends.
- **B** the band members' parents.
- **C** people in the neighbourhood.

3 Choose **all** that apply. A poster about an event must include
- **A** the history of the event organisers.
- **B** what is happening.
- **C** where and when it's on.
- **D** why the event is happening.
- **E** how many people are invited.
- **F** who to contact for further information.

4 Which **two** words in the text are the most persuasive?

....

....

5 The photograph is useful for
- **A** deciding if the band members are good musicians.
- **B** deciding how crowded the concert will be.
- **C** seeing what the band members look like.

6 If you lived in Beatie St, Rozelle, would you like to go to the concert? Explain.

....

....

....

Get creative

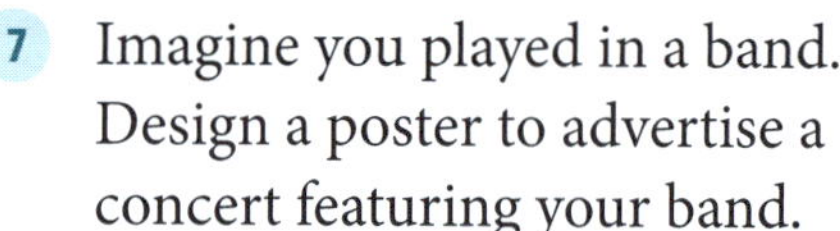

7 Imagine you played in a band. Design a poster to advertise a concert featuring your band.

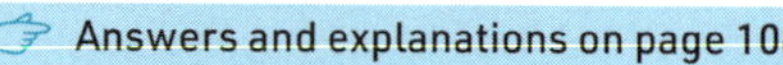

Answers and explanations on page 108

Nerves

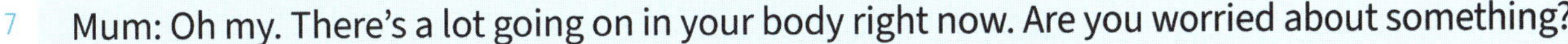

Alex: I feel sick, Mum. I can't go to school.

Mum: You don't have a temperature. You feel cold and clammy but you look flushed. Where do you feel sick?

Alex: In my stomach. I might vomit. Or I might have diarrhoea. My legs feel shaky. I feel dizzy. My heart feels like it's beating really fast.

Mum: Oh my. There's a lot going on in your body right now. Are you worried about something? Those symptoms are all the ways your body reacts to stress or to feeling nervous. Is something happening at school that's bothering you?

Alex: I don't want to go to school.

Mum: Let's just pause and take some deep breaths. Let's breathe in and blow up our tummies like a balloon: 1, 2, 3, 4, 5. Now breathe out 1, 2, 3, 4, 5.

Again.

Again.

Now, tell me. What is worrying you to make your body behave like this?

1 Choose **all** that apply. What are Alex's symptoms?

- **A** flushed
- **B** a temperature
- **C** clammy
- **D** vomiting
- **E** diarrhoea
- **F** shaky legs
- **G** dizziness

2 What does Mum think is wrong with Alex?

- **A** He needs to take deep breaths.
- **B** He is worried about something.
- **C** He has the flu.

3 Deep breaths might help if you

- **A** have diarrhoea.
- **B** are vomiting.
- **C** are nervous.

4 Which is true?

- **A** Alex feels sick.
- **B** Alex is pretending to be sick.
- **C** Alex likes to trick his mum.

5 Mum is

- **A** calm.
- **B** worried.
- **C** angry.

6 Why might Alex be worried about school? ....

....

....

Answers and explanations on page 108

SPELLING

Write the correct spelling of the underlined words in questions 1–4.

1 You don't have a temprature.

2 I mite vomit.

3 Take a deep breathe.

4 Is somthing happening at school?

5 Write three words from the word family that includes **sick**.

VOCABULARY

6 Circle the answer that has the nearest meaning to the underlined word.

I feel sick.

A diseased B stressed
C ill D awkward

7 Write a word from the text to match the meaning.

when your skin feels damp

8 Add a word from the text to complete the sentence.

If you need to go to the toilet a lot, you might have .

9 Circle the word that does **not** belong.

A shaky B wobbly
C trembly D sturdy

GRAMMAR

10 Complete the sentence with a common noun from the text.

His is beating really fast.

11 Choose the correct saying verb to complete the sentence.

'Let's take deep breaths,' Mum.

A quoted
B asked
C advised
D yelled

12 Write a prepositional phrase from the text that tells **where**.

Mum asked if something was happening

.

13 Choose a pronoun to correctly complete the sentence.

Listen to your mum. will tell you what to do.

A Her B She
C We D They

PUNCTUATION

Rewrite the sentences correctly.

14 now breathe out 1 2 3 4 5

15 mum thinks alex has a problem at school

Answers and explanations on page 108

TEXTS IN CONTEXT

Nerves

Alex: I feel sick, Mum. I can't go to school.

Mum: You don't have a temperature. You feel cold and clammy but you look flushed. Where do you feel sick?

Alex: In my stomach. I might vomit. Or I might have diarrhoea. My legs feel shaky. I feel dizzy. My heart feels like it's beating really fast.

Mum: Oh my. There's a lot going on in your body right now. Are you worried about something? Those symptoms are all the ways your body reacts to stress or to feeling nervous. Is something happening at school that's bothering you?

Alex: I don't want to go to school.

Mum: Let's just pause and take some deep breaths. Let's breathe in and blow up our tummies like a balloon: 1, 2, 3, 4, 5. Now breathe out 1, 2, 3, 4, 5.

Again.

Again.

Now, tell me. What is worrying you to make your body behave like this?

1 In the text, Mum's purpose is to
- **A** make Alex breathe properly.
- **B** tell readers about Alex.
- **C** find out why Alex feels sick.

2 Who might find this text relevant?
- **A** parents with sick children
- **B** children who are so worried about something they feel sick
- **C** doctors, nurses and teachers

3 Add a simile from the text.

Let's breathe in and blow up our tummies

....

....

4 The text includes medical terms. Write **two** of them.

....

....

5 In the photograph Mum is feeling Alex's forehead to see if he
- **A** is flushed.
- **B** is clammy or has a high temperature.
- **C** has a fast heart rate.

6 Have you ever felt any of Alex's symptoms? Explain.

....

....

....

....

7 Write a story that might explain Alex's symptoms.

Answers and explanations on page 108

Is that you, Dad?

The children's chairs floated above the floor. Books floated to them from off the shelves. The children scanned the pages for the spell they needed to help their dad. Unwanted books fluttered to the floor beneath them.

The children's dad had turned into a dog. (They were almost positive.) Dad was missing and an odd sort of dog had turned up. It seemed to understand what they said. If they asked it questions, it barked once to answer 'yes' and twice to answer 'no'. They had also tested it by telling it to please fetch them one blue sock and one yellow sock from Dad's bedroom. It did, then it sat in their father's seat to watch TV and it kept hold of the remote control—very Dad-like. But it didn't make them do their homework so they rather liked this dog-dad.

They needn't hurry to find the right spell.

1. The children are looking for
   - **A** a book.
   - **B** a spell.
   - **C** their dad.

2. Choose **all** that apply.
   Books .... around them.
   - **A** flew
   - **B** floated
   - **C** fluttered

3. The children think the dog is
   - **A** clever.
   - **B** cute.
   - **C** cunning.

4. Which clue seems most Dad-like?
   - **A** guarding the remote control
   - **B** fetching coloured socks
   - **C** being an odd sort of dog

5. The dog
   - **A** can speak English.
   - **B** seems to understand English.
   - **C** wants to learn English.

6. Which clues in the text lead the children to think that the dog is their dad?

   ....

   ....

Answers and explanations on pages 108–109

SPELLING

Write the correct spelling of the underlined words in questions 1–4.

1 Books flutterd to the floor.

2 Books floated off the shelfs.

3 The dog had to fetch sum socks.

4 The children had homewerk to do.

5 Write three words from the word family that includes **questions**.

VOCABULARY

6 Circle the answer that has the nearest meaning to the underlined word.

The dog had to fetch socks.

A obtain
B carry
C find
D go get

7 Write a word from the text to match the meaning.

searched through the pages in a book

8 Name the item in the text that controls a device from a distance.

9 Circle the word that does **not** belong.

A disappeared
B missing
C dissolved
D vanished

GRAMMAR

10 Complete the sentence with a common noun from the text.

The children sat on ______.

11 Choose the correct saying verb to complete the sentence.

The children ______ the dog some questions.

A questioned
B told
C asked
D said

12 Write a prepositional phrase from the text that tells **where**.

The socks were fetched ______.

13 Choose a pronoun to correctly complete the sentence.

The children scanned the pages for the spell ______ needed.

A them
B they
C we
D us

PUNCTUATION

Rewrite the sentences correctly.

14 is that dad

15 the dog sat in their fathers seat

Answers and explanations on page 109

Is that you, Dad?

❶ The children's chairs floated above the floor. Books floated to them from off the shelves. The children scanned the pages for the spell they needed to help their dad. Unwanted books fluttered to the floor beneath them.

❷ The children's dad had turned into a dog. (They were almost positive.) Dad was missing and an odd sort of dog had turned up. It seemed to understand what they said. If they asked it questions, it barked once to answer 'yes' and twice to answer 'no'. They had also tested it by telling it to please fetch them one blue sock and one yellow sock from Dad's bedroom. It did, then it sat in their father's seat to watch TV and it kept hold of the remote control—very Dad-like. But it didn't make them do their homework so they rather liked this dog-dad.

❸ They needn't hurry to find the right spell.

1 The text is part of a
- **A** report on a missing dad.
- **B** story about a missing dad.
- **C** recount of events in the children's lives.

2 Which is the most likely audience for this text?
- **A** teachers
- **B** adults
- **C** children

3 'They were almost positive' (line 5) means
- **A** it's true.
- **B** it's likely to be true.
- **C** it's probably not true.

4 Choose **all** that apply. The photo supports paragraph
- **A** one.
- **B** two.
- **C** three.

5 How worried are the children about their father?
- **A** extremely worried
- **B** very worried
- **C** not worried that much

6 The atmosphere in the photo is
- **A** scary.
- **B** calm.
- **C** panicked.

Get creative

7 What adventures could you have with a dog-dad? Write a story.

Answers and explanations on page 109

Just joking

Emma could hear the children's whispers behind her. Rose was whispering to Trent and Erik. Emma knew they were talking about her.

Rose was the problem. She called Emma stupid names to make the other children laugh about Emma's hair. She made fun of Emma's clothes on free-dress day and Emma's drawings in art. She told lies about Emma. She told the other children not to play with Emma or sit with her. She'd say something mean and then say 'Just joking' but she wasn't. Some of Emma's so-called friends would giggle. It would hurt Emma's feelings but she'd try to laugh at the 'joke'.

Emma's Mum said that Rose was jealous. Rose wanted to make Emma feel bad so that she could feel better about herself. This did not make a lot of sense to Rose but it helped that her mother seemed to understand her problem.

Rose's bullying used to make Emma feel sad but now it made her mad.

1 In the photo

- **A** Emma is whispering about Rose.
- **B** Rose is whispering to Trent and Erik.
- **C** Emma is whispering to Trent and Erik.
- **D** Rose is whispering about Emma's bullying.

2 Rose's bullying now makes Emma feel

- **A** sad.
- **B** glad.
- **C** bad.
- **D** mad.

3 Who is Rose likely to be jealous of?

- **A** Emma's Mum
- **B** Emma's friends
- **C** Emma
- **D** other children at school

4 A 'so-called' friend is a person who

- **A** is a true friend.
- **B** you can trust to be your loyal friend.
- **C** is meant to be a friend but is not acting like a friend.
- **D** calls you a friend.

5 Choose **all** that apply. What does Rose tease Emma about?

- **A** her clothes
- **B** her drawings
- **C** her friends
- **D** her appearance

6 Is Rose really 'Just joking' about Emma?

- **A** Yes. She likes to make children laugh and have fun.
- **B** Yes. Rose has fun with jokes.
- **C** No. It's not a joke if Rose says it's not.
- **D** No. She only says 'Just joking' as an excuse for being mean.

7 Choose **all** that apply. Trent and Erik should

- **A** not listen to nasty comments.
- **B** tell a teacher about Rose's behaviour.
- **C** defend Emma as a friend.
- **D** choose Rose as a friend.
- **E** tell Rose they don't want to hear anything mean.
- **F** tell Emma to say mean things to Rose.

Answers and explanations on page 109

Each sentence has one word that is incorrect. Write the correct spelling of each underlined word.

1 Dad was <u>wispering</u>.

....

2 Is Mum <u>jokeing</u>?

....

3 When are your <u>frends</u> coming over?

....

4 It's fun to giggle and <u>larf</u>.

....

5 She might be <u>jellis</u> of her baby sister.

....

Read the text below. Choose the correct verb or verb group to correctly complete each sentence.

> The children ......(6)...... the race.
>
> 'Congratulations Ella,' said Alejandro. 'You ......(7)...... well to come second behind Zoi.'
>
> 'Thanks. I'm happy. Zoi ......(8)...... a great runner,' said Ella.

6 **A** had finished **B** were finished **C** is finishing **D** are finished

7 **A** running **B** could run **C** ran **D** was running

8 **A** are **B** is **C** was **D** am

9 Which word is a common noun in the sentence?

'Put your dirty clothes over there, Timmy,' said Trevor.

A dirty **B** clothes **C** there **D** Timmy

10 Which word is a relating (being) verb in the sentence?

Ned is good at drawing dogs.

A dogs
B drawing
C is
D good

11 Which word or phrase tells where?

The children sat under the tree to eat lunch.

A sat
B children
C under the tree
D lunch

12 Which pronoun correctly completes the sentence?

The children ate lunch quickly. .... wanted to play tag.

A We **B** They **C** It **D** Them

13 Which sentence is punctuated correctly?

A The child wasnt joking.
B The joke's were not funny.
C The child was'nt joking after all.
D Emma wasn't joking.

14 Which sentence is punctuated correctly?

A Don't hurt his feeling's.
B she'd be happy to join in.
C The teacher could hear the children's laughter.
D She'd like a sandwich for lunch.

Answers and explanations on page 109

Rock pools

Rock pools are formed at the seaside when the tide goes out. Creatures such as crabs, fish, sea stars, limpets and sea snails can be seen in rock pools.

Rock pool rules

1. Look but don't touch.
Why? A rock pool might shelter a blue-ringed octopus. It burrows under the sand and is hard to see but it is dangerous. It is poisonous. It is usually brown but shows blue rings when it feels threatened.

2. Leave everything as you found it.
Why? Be kind to the creatures that shelter there. Do not disturb them or harm them or their home.

3. Take nothing away.
Why? Rock-pool creatures suffer and die when taken out of their environment. They need clean, tidal salt water to survive. You can't give them that in a bucket or at your home so they die.

1 What dangerous animal might hide in a rock pool?
A a limpet **B** a crab **C** a blue-ringed octopus

2 A blue-ringed octopus
A only has blue rings when it thinks it's in danger.
B has blue rings when it's dangerous.
C has brown and blue stripes and is poisonous.

3 How is a rock pool made?
A The tide goes out and washes the rock pools away.
B The tide goes out at the beach and leaves puddles in the sand.
C The tide goes out and pools of water are left in the rocks.

4 What happens to sea creatures taken away from the sea?
A They don't like to be touched. **B** They can live in a bucket. **C** They die.

5 Choose **all** that apply. Why is it not good to move rocks around in a rock pool?
A You will disturb animals in the rock pool.
B You might disturb a blue-ringed octopus.
C Some animals hide under rocks.

6 What does the writer want people to do? ....

....

Answers and explanations on page 109

SPELLING

Write the correct spelling of the underlined words in questions 1–4.

1 An octopuss has eight legs.

....

2 Don't tuch the animals.

....

3 A sea star is a rock-pool creeture.

....

4 Look after the enviramænt.

....

5 Write three words from the word family that includes **dangerous**.

....

....

VOCABULARY

6 Circle the answer that has the nearest meaning to the underlined word.

Rock pools shelter many creatures.

A hide **B** protect
C shade **D** guard

7 Write a word from the text to match the meaning.

when something is deadly or can make you very sick

....

8 Add a word from the text to complete the sentence.

Rock .... are formed when the tide goes out.

9 Circle the word or word group that does **not** belong.

A mess up **B** interfere with
C disturb **D** look at

GRAMMAR

10 Complete the sentence with an adjective from the text.

A garden snail is not a .... creature.

11 Choose the correct verb group to complete the sentence.

The creatures .... clean, tidal salt water.

A are having
B must have
C had needed
D were needing

12 Complete the sentence with a phrase that tell **where**.

The blue-ringed octopus lives ....

....

13 Choose a conjunction to correctly join the clauses.

It is dangerous .... it is poisonous.

A and **B** so
C because **D** but

PUNCTUATION

Rewrite the sentences correctly.

14 why cant we touch things in a rock pool

....

....

....

15 its better to leave things alone

....

....

Answers and explanations on page 109

Rock pools

Rock pools are formed at the seaside when the tide goes out. Creatures such as crabs, fish, sea stars, limpets and sea snails can be seen in rock pools.

Rock pool rules

1. Look but don't touch.
Why? A rock pool might shelter a blue-ringed octopus. It burrows under the sand and is hard to see but it is dangerous. It is poisonous. It is usually brown but shows blue rings when it feels threatened.

2. Leave everything as you found it.
Why? Be kind to the creatures that shelter there. Do not disturb them or harm them or their home.

3. Take nothing away.
Why? Rock-pool creatures suffer and die when taken out of their environment. They need clean, tidal salt water to survive. You can't give them that in a bucket or at your home so they die.

1 The purpose of the text is to
- **A** explain why rock pools are important.
- **B** instruct what to do at rock pools.
- **C** describe rock pools to readers.

2 The main audience for the rules would be
- **A** teachers.
- **B** scientists.
- **C** children.

3 The structure of the text is
- **A** a heading, a subheading and rules for rock pools.
- **B** an orientation to rock pools then three rules that describe rock pools.
- **C** an introduction then three rules plus the reasons for each rule.

4 Circle the technical terms in the text.

5 Find **two** words in the text that tell you the writer worries about the welfare of animals in rock pools.

....

....

6 What do you think of the behaviour of the children in the photo?

....

....

....

7 Describe a place in the natural environment where you think it's important to look but not touch.

Answers and explanations on pages 109–110

READING AND COMPREHENSION

Beach safety

❶ At the beach, always swim between the red and yellow flags. The red and yellow flags show you that lifeguards are on duty at that part of the beach. Lifeguards put the flags out where it is safest for swimmers. If you get into difficulty, raise your hand and a lifeguard will help you. If there are no red and yellow flags, DO NOT SWIM.

❷ A red flag means the beach is closed. There might be a dangerous rip that can sweep swimmers out to sea. Or there might be huge waves that could dump you on a sandbank.

❸ A red-and-white flag means 'Get out of the water now.' This flag is used when a shark has been spotted.

❹ Sometimes there are bluebottles at the beach. Bluebottles are creatures that float. The wind pushes them across the sea. They have tentacles that sting their prey. If you get stung, wash the area with sea water. Make sure the tentacles come off. Then soak the area in hot water or have a hot bath. Hot water is best for the pain. If there's no hot water, use ice.

1 Where should you swim?
- **A** where you see a lifeguard
- **B** between the red flags
- **C** between the red and yellow flags

2 What do you do if you get into difficulty while swimming?
- **A** Call your parents.
- **B** Yell to a friend.
- **C** Raise your hand.

3 How do bluebottles hurt you?
- **A** Their tentacles sting you.
- **B** Their tentacles wrap around you.
- **C** They attack you with their tentacles.

4 Make sure the tentacles come off so
- **A** you can soak your arm in hot water.
- **B** they don't strangle you.
- **C** they don't keep stinging you.

5 The most common safety risk at a beach is
- **A** a shark.
- **B** a rip.
- **C** bluebottles.

6 What is the purpose of the flags at the beach?

....

....

Answers and explanations on page 110

SPELLING

Write the correct spelling of the underlined words in questions 1–4.

1 Lifegards save lives.

2 A red flag means the beach is clozed.

3 Huje waves can dump you.

4 A rip can sweep swimmars out to sea.

5 Write three words from the word family that includes **carries**.

VOCABULARY

6 Circle the answer that has the nearest meaning to the underlined word.

A shark was spotted so the red and white flag went up.

A seen B caught
C painted D hunted

7 Write a word from the text to match the meaning.

animals hunted for food

8 Add a word from the text to complete the sentence.

Bluebottles have stinging .

9 Circle the word that does **not** belong.

A difficulty B emergency
C trouble D enjoyment

GRAMMAR

10 Complete the sentence with an adjective from the text.

A rip can sweep you out to sea.

11 Choose the correct verb group to complete the sentence.

A lifeguard you if you raise your hand.

A used to help
B will help
C did help
D is helping.

12 Complete the sentence with a prepositional phrase that tells **where**.

Always swim .

13 Choose a conjunction to correctly join the clauses.

Hot water is best for a bluebottle sting , if there's no hot water, use ice.

A and B so
C because D but

PUNCTUATION

Rewrite the sentences correctly.

14 what is best for a bluebottle sting

15 lifeguards helped matilda

Answers and explanations on page 110

TEXTS IN CONTEXT

Beach safety

❶ At the beach, always swim between the red and yellow flags. The red and yellow flags show you that lifeguards are on duty at that part of the beach. Lifeguards put the flags out where it is safest for swimmers. If you get into difficulty, raise your hand and a lifeguard will help you. If there are no red and yellow flags, DO NOT SWIM.

❷ A red flag means the beach is closed. There might be a dangerous rip that can sweep swimmers out to sea. Or there might be huge waves that could dump you on a sandbank.

❸ A red-and-white flag means 'Get out of the water now.' This flag is used when a shark has been spotted.

❹ Sometimes there are bluebottles at the beach. Bluebottles are creatures that float. The wind pushes them across the sea. They have tentacles that sting their prey. If you get stung, wash the area with sea water. Make sure the tentacles come off. Then soak the area in hot water or have a hot bath. Hot water is best for the pain. If there's no hot water, use ice.

1 The purpose of the text is to
- **A** give instructions about swimming at the beach.
- **B** give information about safety at the beach.
- **C** explain about beach flags.

2 The author writes
- **A** about people at the beach.
- **B** to you as a possible beachgoer.
- **C** about him- or herself at the beach.

3 You know a bluebottle sting hurts because
- **A** they sting their prey.
- **B** you'll need hot water or ice.
- **C** the text tells you what to do for pain.

4 Link the subject to the paragraph numbers.

Paragraph 1	**A** bluebottles
Paragraph 2	**B** red and yellow flags
Paragraph 3	**C** red-and-white flags
Paragraph 4	**D** red flags

5 Choose **all** that apply. What would a lifeguard do if someone raised an arm?
- **A** Swim out to help them.
- **B** Call out to check they are safe.
- **C** Leave them alone.

6 Choose **all** that apply. What might a lifeguard think about people swimming outside the red and yellow flags?
- **A** They are risking their safety.
- **B** They are smart people.
- **C** They should learn what the flags mean.

Get creative

7 Write some safety advice for somewhere that you know such as your home, your school, your classroom or a park.

Answers and explanations on page 110

Hi Barbang

My class went to see the sand sculptures in the city today. The theme of the event was extinction.

250 tonnes of sand had been delivered to the site from a quarry. The sand arrived in blocks. It was compacted so it could be carved. Twenty-five professional artists worked for ten days to create the sculptures. A biodegradable glue was used to help the sculptures last—for a while anyway.

Our class voted on our favourite. The winner was one with dinosaurs. That wasn't my favourite. I liked the West African Black rhinoceros sculpture best. You'd have loved it too. My teacher said there used to be lots of those rhinos across Africa but they were declared extinct in 2011. That's so sad.

When I grow up I am going to be a sand sculptor.

Love Gillen ☾ XXX

1 The class went to see
- **A** dinosaurs.
- **B** sand sculptures.
- **C** Barbang.

2 The sand for the sculptures came from
- **A** the beach.
- **B** near the sea.
- **C** a quarry.

3 All of the sculptures would have shown
- **A** large animals.
- **B** extinct animals.
- **C** how sand is delivered.

4 A biodegradable glue
- **A** is a good glue for paper.
- **B** helps the sculptures last forever.
- **C** holds the sculptures together temporarily.

5 If the sand hadn't been compacted
- **A** it would not have been able to be delivered.
- **B** it would not have been able to be carved.
- **C** the sculptors would have taken longer to finish.

6 Why might Gillen want to be a sand sculptor?

....

....

Answers and explanations on page 110

SPELLING

Write the correct spelling of the underlined words in questions 1–4.

1 The class saw sculpchas.

2 The theme was all about exstingshun.

3 The artists werked for ten days.

4 We votid on our favourite.

5 Write three words from the word family that includes **delivered**.

VOCABULARY

6 Circle the answer that has the nearest meaning to the underlined word.

The sculptures were carved from sand.

A shaped
B compacted
C made
D cut

7 Write a word from the text to match the meaning.

a person who paints, draws, sculpts or does other creative works

8 Add a word or words from the text to complete the sentence.

'I thought the ______ sculpture was best,' said Gillen.

9 Circle the word that does **not** belong.

A declared
B announced
C predicted
D proclaimed

GRAMMAR

10 Complete the sentence with an adjective from the text.

Twenty-five ______ artists worked on the sculptures.

11 Choose the correct verb group to complete the sentence.

The black rhino ______ extinct in 2011.

A has been declared
B will declare
C was declared
D did declare

12 Complete the sentence with a prepositional phrase that tells **where**.

The sand came ______.

13 Choose a conjunction to correctly join the clauses.

The sand was compacted ______ it could be carved.

A and
B so
C because
D but

PUNCTUATION

Rewrite the sentences correctly.

14 gillen liked the west african black rhino sculpture best

15 the dinosaur sculpture wasnt her favourite

Answers and explanations on page 110

Hi Barbang

My class went to see the sand sculptures in the city today. The theme of the event was extinction.

250 tonnes of sand had been delivered to the site from a quarry. The sand arrived in blocks. It was compacted so it could be carved. Twenty-five professional artists worked for ten days to create the sculptures. A biodegradable glue was used to help the sculptures last—for a while anyway.

Our class voted on our favourite. The winner was one with dinosaurs. That wasn't my favourite. I liked the West African Black rhinoceros sculpture best. You'd have loved it too. My teacher said there used to be lots of those rhinos across Africa but they were declared extinct in 2011. That's so sad.

When I grow up I am going to be a sand sculptor.

Love Gillen ☾ XXX

1 Gillen's purpose is to
- A recount events on a class excursion.
- B communicate with someone she knows.
- C describe her favourite sand sculpture.

2 Choose **all** that apply. The text is
- A friendly.
- B formal.
- C chatty.
- D informal.

3 The text has an
- A orientation, complication and resolution.
- B introduction, information and concluding statement.
- C introduction, persuasion and conclusion.

4 Barbang and Gillen are words from the Yugara Aboriginal language. Barbang means grandmother. What might Gillen mean in Yugara?
- A love
- B moon
- C sand

5 Which is more definite?
- A I'd like to be
- B I am going to be
- C I think I'll be

6 Why didn't the West African Black rhinoceros sculpture win the class vote?
- A because it was Gillen's favourite
- B because that animal is now extinct
- C because more children in the class preferred the dinosaur sculpture

7 If you were a sand sculptor at the event, which animal would you have sculpted? Explain.

Answers and explanations on page 110

Hugo meets Uncle Norman

Hugo stood beside his mother and looked at the house. This was the address Uncle Norman had sent them. Hugo would need to live here for the next three months while his mother went overseas for her job. He could not believe his mother wanted to leave him here with an Uncle he had never met. It seemed that it must be a joke.

But it wasn't.

'It looks a bit scary,' said his mum.

It looks very scary! thought Hugo.

'But Uncle Norman is a sweetie,' continued his mum.

Why would Uncle Norman want to live in a haunted house? thought Hugo, looking at the black animals around the house and the dead trees.

Mum continued, 'I know you'll get on like a house on fire.'

That doesn't sound good, thought Hugo. He didn't want to be on fire.

Mum stood still, looking at the house. It had been 20 years since she'd seen her brother. Hugo watched her. He was worried. Mum didn't look very confident.

Neither of them moved.

1 Mum
- **A** met Norman 20 years ago.
- **B** says Norman is Hugo's brother.
- **C** hasn't seen Norman in 20 years.

2 Mum had
- **A** never seen the house before.
- **B** lived in the house with Norman when they were children.
- **C** lived with Hugo here before.

3 Which statement is true?
- **A** Hugo's mother lives overseas.
- **B** Hugo had never met Uncle Norman.
- **C** Hugo's mum was only joking about leaving him.

4 Mum
- **A** hopes Hugo is still a sweetie.
- **B** knows Norman is a sweetie.
- **C** hopes Norman is not scared.

5 Is Hugo's mother happy about leaving Hugo?
- **A** Yes. She thinks he'll have a great time.
- **B** No. She thinks the house is haunted.
- **C** Not really. She is having doubts about it.

6 Describe what mum might be thinking or feeling when she 'stood still, looking at the house' (line 15).

Answers and explanations on page 110

SPELLING

Write the correct spelling of the underlined words in questions 1–4.

1 That doe'snt sound good.

....

2 Hugo could not beleeve it.

....

3 The adress might be wrong.

....

4 Hugo was wurreed.

....

5 Write three words from the word family that includes **believe**.

....

....

....

VOCABULARY

6 Circle the answer that has the nearest meaning to the underlined word.

The house looked scary.

A dark B old
C frightening D ruined

7 Write words from the text to match the meaning.

A house said to have ghosts is said to be

....

8 Add a word from the text to complete the sentence.

Your mother's brother is your

....

9 Circle the word that does **not** belong.

A confident B undecided
C certain D definite

GRAMMAR

10 Complete the sentence with an adjective from the text.

There were .... animals near the house.

11 Choose the correct verb group to complete the sentence.

I know you .... your uncle.

A are liking
B had liked
C will like
D would like

12 Complete the sentence with a prepositional phrase that tells **where**.

Hugo stood ....

....

13 Choose a conjunction to correctly join the clauses.

Hugo was worried .... Mum did not look confident.

A and B so
C because D but

PUNCTUATION

Rewrite the sentences correctly.

14 it wasnt a joke

....

....

15 it looks scary said mum

....

....

Answers and explanations on page 111

Hugo meets Uncle Norman

Hugo stood beside his mother and looked at the house. This was the address Uncle Norman had sent them. Hugo would need to live here for the next three months while his mother went overseas for her job. He could not believe his mother wanted to leave him here with an Uncle he had never met. It seemed that it must be a joke.

But it wasn't.

'It looks a bit scary,' said his mum.

It looks very scary! thought Hugo.

'But Uncle Norman is a sweetie,' continued his mum.

Why would Uncle Norman want to live in a haunted house? thought Hugo, looking at the black animals around the house and the dead trees.

Mum continued, 'I know you'll get on like a house on fire.'

That doesn't sound good, thought Hugo. He didn't want to be on fire.

Mum stood still, looking at the house. It had been twenty years since she'd seen her brother. Hugo watched her. He was worried. Mum didn't look very confident.

Neither of them moved.

1. The text is part of a story. Its purpose is to
   - A inform.
   - B entertain.
   - C persuade.

2. The text is written for
   - A teenagers.
   - B very young children.
   - C children around Hugo's age.

3. The expression 'you'll get on like a house on fire' (line 13) means
   - A one of you will annoy the other.
   - B you'll get on really well.
   - C you'll hate each other.

4. Which is true?
   - A Mum talks and then waits for Hugo to answer.
   - B Mum is talking while Hugo is only thinking answers.
   - C Mum and Hugo are having a conversation.

5. Choose **all** that apply. Which things in the photo make the setting look scary?
   - A black birds (ravens)
   - B black cat
   - C bats
   - D dead tree branches
   - E a full moon
   - F an old house with attic windows

6. If you were Hugo, would you want to live in the house for three months while your mum went overseas? Explain your answer.

....

....

7. Write what you think happens to Hugo in the story.

Answers and explanations on page 111

Look after your skin

My name is Abigail. My dad had skin cancer. He had a melanoma on his nose. Melanoma is the third most common kind of skin cancer and the most deadly. A melanoma can kill you. My dad was lucky because the doctor cut out his melanoma when it was only small and it hadn't spread anywhere in his body. Australians get more skin cancer than anywhere else in the world because of our sunshine.

To help prevent skin cancer, the Cancer Council says to **slip, slop, slap, seek** and **slide**.

1. **Slip** on clothing that covers your skin.
2. **Slop** on some SPF30+ sunscreen.
3. **Slap** on a broad-brimmed hat.
4. **Seek** out some shade. (**Stay** indoors between 11 am and 3 pm. That's when the sun is at its strongest and is most damaging for your skin.)
5. **Slide** on sunglasses to protect your eyes.

Do these five things and you will protect your skin throughout your life.

1 The sun can cause ....

2 What is the most deadly kind of skin cancer? ....

3 Where can you seek shade? ....

4 Which clothing is best for sun protection?

A a long-sleeved shirt　　B shorts　　C a T-shirt

5 Choose the best answer. Abigail's hat is good because

A it protects her ears.　　B it protects her nose　　C it is broad-brimmed.

6 Why did Abigail think her dad was lucky?

....

....

....

Answers and explanations on page 111

SPELLING

Write the correct spelling of the underlined words in questions 1–4.

1 Prevent skin canser.

2 Protekt your skin.

3 Australans have to look after their skin.

4 The cancer had'nt spread.

5 Write three words from the word family that includes **damaging**.

VOCABULARY

6 Circle the answer that has the nearest meaning to the underlined word.

The sun can damage your skin.

A protect B burn
C injure D benefit

7 Write words from the text to match the meaning.

to keep something safe from harm

8 Add a word from the text to complete the sentence.

The cancer did not spread through Dad's ______.

9 Circle the word that does **not** belong.

A strongest B harshest
C luckiest D deadliest

GRAMMAR

10 Complete the sentence with an adjective from the text.

The sun is ______ between 11 am and 3 pm.

11 Choose the correct verb group to complete the sentence.

You ______ your skin for life.

A is protecting
B are protected
C did protect
D need to protect

12 Complete the sentence with a prepositional phrase that tells **where**.

The cancer had not spread ______.

13 Choose a conjunction to correctly join the clauses.

Cancer is deadly ______ protect your skin.

A and B so
C because D but

PUNCTUATION

Rewrite the sentences correctly.

14 thats when the sun is strongest

15 the sun can be deadly in australia

Answers and explanations on page 111

TEXTS IN CONTEXT

Look after your skin

My name is Abigail. My dad had skin cancer. He had a melanoma on his nose. Melanoma is the third most common kind of skin cancer and the most deadly. A melanoma can kill you. My dad was lucky because the doctor cut out his melanoma when it was only small and it hadn't spread anywhere in his body. Australians get more skin cancer than anywhere else in the world because of our sunshine.

To help prevent skin cancer, the Cancer Council says to **slip, slop, slap, seek** and **slide.**

1. **Slip** on clothing that covers your skin.
2. **Slop** on some SPF30+ sunscreen.
3. **Slap** on a broad-brimmed hat.
4. **Seek** out some shade. (**Stay** indoors between 11am and 3pm. That's when the sun is at its strongest and is most damaging for your skin.)
5. **Slide** on sunglasses to protect your eyes.

Do these five things and you will protect your skin throughout your life.

1 The purpose of the text is to tell you
- **A** that the sun can be dangerous.
- **B** about Abigail's dad.
- **C** how to be safe from the sun.

2 Who wrote the text?
- **A** a skin-cancer expert
- **B** a doctor
- **C** the girl in the photo

3 Identify the alliteration in the list numbered 1–5. Circle the **six** doing verbs that start with the same letter. Circle other words in the list that also start with that letter.

4 The structure of the text is
- **A** a description of Dad, a list of instructions then a final instruction.
- **B** an introduction, a list of commands then a resolution.
- **C** an introduction, a list of commands then a conclusion.

5 Why do you think the writer cares if you protect your skin?

....

....

....

6 Is sitting under a tree good enough to comply with the instruction to stay indoors between 11 am and 3 pm?
- **A** Yes. Shade keeps you out of the sun.
- **B** No, because the sun can still reach you in the shade.
- **C** Yes, if that's the best you can do.

7 Design a sun protection poster that would teach children aged 3–5 how to look after their skin.

Answers and explanations on page 111

We need ants

Ants do many important jobs.

Ants tunnel into the soil. Their tunnels let air and water into the soil.

Some ants help people by eating the eggs and larvae of termites, ticks, flies and cockroaches. Those insects are not wanted in our homes.

Ants carry seeds from place to place. Some plants rely on ants to do this.

Some ants store seeds in their nests. Seeds stored in ant nests are protected from seed-eating insects and harsh weather. Ant nests contain useful nutrients to help seeds sprout and grow. The ants eat some of the sprouting seeds.

Ant waste makes the soil richer. Richer soil helps plants grow well.

Humans have disturbed where ants live. This loss of habitat puts ants at risk of extinction. Some species of ants have already become extinct. Other ant species are endangered. Let's make sure that no more ant species become extinct because plants and people need them.

1 Ant tunnels let .... and .... into the soil.

2 Name **four** insects that people don't want in their homes.

....

....

3 The green shoot growing from a seed is called a
A baby tree.
B root.
C sprout.

4 Ants can become extinct when
A they can't find any seeds for their nests.
B their habitat is destroyed.
C people kill them with insect spray.

5 What is ant waste?
A poo
B garbage
C unwanted seeds

6 How are ants like farmers? ....

....

Answers and explanations on page 111

SPELLING

Write the correct spelling of the underlined words in questions 1–4.

1 Ants make tunnils.

2 Ants can eat termite larvay.

3 Ants spred seeds.

4 Peeple need ants.

5 Write three words from the word family that includes **grow**.

VOCABULARY

6 Circle the answer that has the nearest meaning to the underlined word.

Ant nests protect seeds from harsh conditions.

A difficult
B ordinary
C regular
D weather

7 Write words from the text to match the meaning.

young insects hatched from eggs

8 Add a word from the text to complete the sentence.

Some ant species are extinct. Others are .

9 Circle the word that does **not** belong.

A store
B keep
C use
D save

GRAMMAR

10 Complete the sentence with an adjective from the text.

Ant nests contain nutrients to help seeds sprout.

11 Choose the correct verb group to complete the sentence.

Seeds well in an ant nest.

A used to grow
B is grown
C did grow
D can grow

12 Complete the sentence with a prepositional phrase that tells **where**.

Ant tunnels let water and air .

13 Choose a conjunction to correctly join the clauses.

I love ants they do important jobs for plants.

A and
B so
C because
D but

PUNCTUATION

Rewrite the sentences correctly.

14 lets make sure ants can do their jobs

15 we dont want termites ticks flies and cockroaches in our homes

Answers and explanations on page 111

We need ants

Ants do many important jobs.

Ants tunnel into the soil. Their tunnels let air and water into the soil.

Some ants help people by eating the eggs and larvae of termites, ticks, flies and cockroaches. Those insects are not wanted in our homes.

Ants carry seeds from place to place. Some plants rely on ants to do this.

Some ants store seeds in their nests. Seeds stored in ant nests are protected from seed-eating insects and harsh weather. Ant nests contain useful nutrients to help seeds sprout and grow. The ants eat some of the sprouting seeds.

Ant waste makes the soil richer. Richer soil helps plants grow well.

Humans have disturbed where ants live. This loss of habitat puts ants at risk of extinction. Some species of ants have already become extinct. Other ant species are endangered. Let's make sure that no more ant species become extinct because plants and people need them.

1 The purpose of the text is to
- **A** tell people how to protect ants.
- **B** give information about ants.
- **C** tell people where to find ants.

2 The text is written by someone who
- **A** knows about ants.
- **B** loves ants.
- **C** does not like ants because they bite.

3 The text has
- **A** an orientation then information in order of importance.
- **B** an opening statement, a sequence of events then a conclusion.
- **C** an introduction, a list of points then a concluding statement.

4 Choose **all** that apply. The text includes
- **A** scientific terminology.
- **B** paragraphs.
- **C** a numbered list.
- **D** a heading and subheadings.

5 The writer calls on readers to
- **A** make sure ants can do their jobs.
- **B** make sure no more ants become extinct.
- **C** help plants and people.

6 Choose **all** that apply. Which conditions can be harsh for seeds?
- **A** an ant nest
- **B** a bushfire
- **C** frost
- **D** snow

7 Do some research about an insect that interests you. Write a report.

Answers and explanations on page 112

READING AND COMPREHENSION

Friends

Friends care for one another.
Friends share good times
and troubles.
They help you celebrate.
They feel for you if you are hurt.
They do things with you—
play, explore, climb, laugh
or just sit in silence.
Friends don't lie to you.
They tell the truth,
even if it hurts a bit.
Friends help you belong.
Friends can agree to disagree.
Friends can count on each other.
They don't mind if you make mistakes
now and then.
They don't blame you.
You can trust your friend
to have your back,
stay by your side,
stick up for you
and face the world with you.
It's good to have a friend.
It's good to make new friends.

1. A friend should not
   - **A** lie to you.
   - **B** count on you.
   - **C** trust you.

2. What **four** things does the poet say you can enjoy doing with friends?

   ....

   ....

   ....

   ....

3. How might a friend 'stick up for you' (line 22)?

   ....

   ....

   ....

4. 'Friends help you belong' (line 13).
   What does this mean?
   - **A** When you have a friend, you feel you are part of something.
   - **B** When you have a friend, you belong to the same groups.
   - **C** Friends belong together.

5. The poet
   - **A** probably doesn't have many friends.
   - **B** thinks that true friends are hard to find.
   - **C** seems to understand what friendship means.

6. What sort of truth might 'hurt a little bit?'

   ....

   ....

   ....

   ....

Answers and explanations on page 112

SPELLING

Write the correct spelling of the underlined words in questions 1–4.

1 Friends share trubbles.

....

2 Always tell the trooth.

....

3 Don't hert friends.

....

4 You can fase the world with a friend.

....

5 Write three words from the word family that includes **celebrate**.

....

....

....

VOCABULARY

6 Circle the answer that has the nearest meaning to the underlined word.

Friends don't blame you.

A promote B attack
C reject D condemn

7 Write a word from the text to match the meaning.

to do something enjoyable for a special day

....

8 Add a word from the text to complete the sentence.

Friends can agree to ....

9 Circle the word that does **not** belong.

A trust B believe
C rely D betray

GRAMMAR

10 Complete the sentence with an adjective from the text.

Friends share .... times.

11 Choose the correct verb group to complete the sentence.

Friends .... if you sometimes make mistakes.

A were not minding
B is not minding
C did not mind
D do not mind

12 Complete the sentence with a prepositional phrase that tells **where**.

Friends have your back and stay ....

....

to face the world.

13 Choose a conjunction to correctly join the clauses.

Friends care .... friends share.

A and B so
C because D but

PUNCTUATION

Rewrite the sentences correctly.

14 were good friends

....

....

15 its good to have friends

....

....

Answers and explanations on page 112

TEXTS IN CONTEXT

Friends

Friends care for one another.
Friends share good times
and troubles.
They help you celebrate.
They feel for you if you are hurt.
They do things with you—
play, explore, climb, laugh
or just sit in silence.
Friends don't lie to you.
They tell the truth,
even if it hurts a bit.
Friends help you belong.
Friends can agree to disagree.
Friends can count on each other.
They don't mind if you make mistakes
now and then.
They don't blame you.
You can trust your friend
to have your back,
stay by your side,
stick up for you
and face the world with you.
It's good to have a friend.
It's good to make new friends.

1 The purpose of the poem is to
- **A** give advice about being a good friend.
- **B** persuade people to make friends.
- **C** describe what friends do for one another.

2 The photo shows that the audience for the poem is
- **A** girls.
- **B** boys.
- **C** adults.
- **D** children.

3 Add the rhyming words from the poem.

Friends .... and

friends ....

4 What does 'You can trust your friend / to have your back' (lines 19–20) mean?

....

....

5 'Friends share good times' (line 3)
What might good times be?

....

....

....

6 What might 'troubles' (lines 3–4) include?

....

....

....

Get creative

7 Write a poem about a particular friend or family member who you care about and share things with.

Answers and explanations on page 112

Someone I admire

Aunty Linda plays tennis. She loves it. She says it keeps her fit and she has made many friends because of tennis. Her husband, Uncle Connor, is a volunteer coach at their local tennis club. He says he loves to watch Linda play. He says she has so much fun he can't stop smiling. Tennis makes them both very happy.

Aunty Linda was in a car accident a few years ago. She has paraplegia because of that so she has a sports wheelchair for tennis. She plays with people who have different types of disabilities. Not all of the players are in wheelchairs but everyone has a disability in the lower part of their body such as their spine, hip, leg or foot. Wheelchair tennis players are allowed two bounces of the ball. That's the only rule difference from traditional tennis.

Before her accident Linda never played tennis. Now she plays three times a week at least. When I play against her she always beats me.

By Ingrid, age 7

1 Linda

- **A** was born with paraplegia.
- **B** has paraplegia due to a car accident.
- **C** has paraplegia due to a tennis accident.

2 Wheelchair tennis players can play against

- **A** other wheelchair players only.
- **B** people with disabilities in their lower limbs.
- **C** anyone.

3 The best thing about tennis for Uncle Connor is

- **A** that he can't stop smiling.
- **B** watching Linda beat Ingrid.
- **C** watching Linda have fun.

4 Having paraplegia means that Linda can't use

- **A** one of her arms.
- **B** her legs.
- **C** her feet.

5 Which statements are supported by evidence in the text? Choose **all** that apply.

- **A** Linda's friends play tennis.
- **B** Linda's niece plays tennis.
- **C** Linda's husband can't play tennis.

6 What is the text mainly about?

....

....

Answers and explanations on page 112

SPELLING

Write the correct spelling of the underlined words in questions 1–4.

1 Unkle Connor loves tennis.

....

2 Arnty Linda loves tennis.

....

3 Linda had a car acident.

....

4 Wheelchair tennis has one rool that's different.

....

5 Write three words from the word family that includes **disabilities**.

....

....

....

VOCABULARY

6 Circle the answer that has the nearest meaning to the underlined word.

She has a disability.

A wheelchair B impairment
C condition D illness

7 Write a word from the text to match the meaning.

the usual way something is done

....

8 Add a word from the text to complete the sentence.

Connor is a .... at their tennis club.

9 Circle the word that does **not** belong.

A decision B accident
C disaster D catastrophe

GRAMMAR

10 Complete the sentence with an adjective from the text.

Able-bodied athletes play .... tennis.

11 Choose the correct verb group to complete the sentence.

Before her accident, Linda .... tennis.

A can never play
B should never play
C had never played
D will never play

12 Complete the sentence with a prepositional phrase that tells **where**.

Connor volunteers ....

....

13 Choose a conjunction to correctly join the clauses.

Linda had never played tennis .... now she loves it.

A and B so
C because D but

PUNCTUATION

Rewrite the sentences correctly.

14 linda and connor cant stop smiling

....

....

15 some players have hip leg spine or foot disabilities

....

....

....

Answers and explanations on page 112

Someone I admire

Aunty Linda plays tennis. She loves it. She says it keeps her fit and she has made many friends because of tennis. Her husband, Uncle Connor, is a volunteer coach at their local tennis club. He says he loves to watch Linda play. He says she has so much fun he can't stop smiling. Tennis makes them both very happy.

Aunty Linda was in a car accident a few years ago. She has paraplegia because of that so she has a sports wheelchair for tennis. She plays with people who have different types of disabilities. Not all of the players are in wheelchairs but everyone has a disability in the lower part of their body such as their spine, hip, leg or foot. Wheelchair tennis players are allowed two bounces of the ball. That's the only rule difference from traditional tennis.

Before her accident Linda never played tennis. Now she plays three times a week at least. When I play against her she always beats me.

By Ingrid, age 7

1 The text is
- A about a real person.
- B part of a story.
- C a newspaper report.

2 The writer is
- A jealous of her aunt because she always beats her at tennis.
- B admires her aunt because she has fun and is good at tennis.
- C feels sorry for her aunt because she has to play tennis in a wheelchair.

3 Paragraph one
- A tells about Linda's car accident.
- B tells how to play wheelchair tennis.
- C tells how much Linda likes tennis.

4 Paragraph two tells
- A how to move around if you have paraplegia.
- B about playing tennis with a disability.
- C about Linda's car accident.

5 Choose **all** that apply. In the photo Linda looks
- A sad.
- B fit.
- C angry.
- D lonely.
- E happy.
- F athletic.

6 Why do you think Ingrid chose to write her text about Linda and tennis?

....

....

....

....

Get creative

7 Write a text about someone you admire. Include a photo if possible.

Answers and explanations on page 112

Plastic problem

Jeremy: Dad, I can't take plastic to school anymore. We learned about plastic pollution in class. It's bad for the environment. It's everywhere. It gets washed or blown into rivers and the ocean and it stays there forever. It just gets broken down into smaller and smaller pieces. Fish think it's food. Then people eat fish and don't know they are eating plastic.

Dad: Yes. I know. It's a huge problem.

Jeremy: Birds and other sea animals end up eating plastic too, not just fish.

Dad: Yes. Animals die because they've eaten plastic. It gets caught in their stomachs. They can't digest it. They starve to death. Birds and whales have been found dead and their stomachs are full of plastic. It's awful.

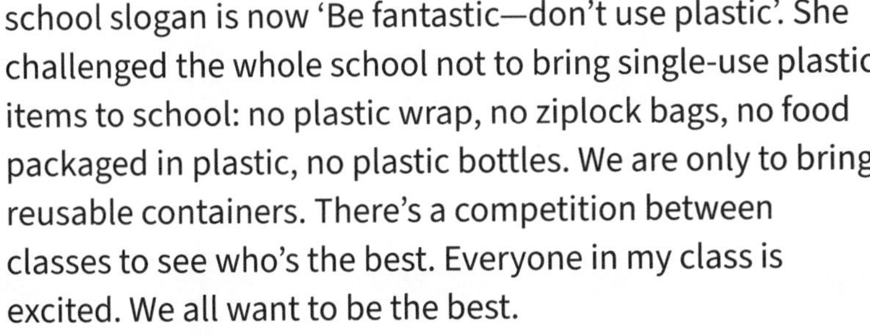
Jeremy: Our Principal Ms Wallace said in assembly that our school slogan is now 'Be fantastic—don't use plastic'. She challenged the whole school not to bring single-use plastic items to school: no plastic wrap, no ziplock bags, no food packaged in plastic, no plastic bottles. We are only to bring reusable containers. There's a competition between classes to see who's the best. Everyone in my class is excited. We all want to be the best.

A black swan trying to eat plastic pollution because it thinks it's food

Dad: Fantastic!

1 Write the new school slogan.

....

....

2 Where did Jeremy learn about plastic pollution?

- **A** in assembly
- **B** from his dad
- **C** from Ms Wallace
- **D** in class

3 Animals eat plastic because

- **A** it's tasty.
- **B** they think it's food.
- **C** there's nothing else to eat.
- **D** they are hungry.

4 How does plastic get in the ocean?

- **A** Animals carry it there.
- **B** The wind carries it.
- **C** Rain washes it down roads and into gutters.
- **D** People drop it when they litter.

5 Jeremy's class wants to be the best at

- **A** winning the competition.
- **B** reusing plastic.
- **C** bringing reusable lunch boxes to school.
- **D** not using plastic.

6 Choose **all** that apply. Plastic harms

- **A** fish and other animals.
- **B** birds.
- **C** oceans and rivers.
- **D** people.

7 Choose **all** that apply. The photo is meant to make readers feel

- **A** angry.
- **B** sad.
- **C** inspired.
- **D** pleased.

Answers and explanations on pages 112–113

Each sentence has one word that is incorrect. Write the correct spelling of the underlined words in the boxes.

1 The Principal spoke to children.

[ ]

2 Plastic is evrywere.

[ ]

3 Don't bring packiged food to school.

[ ]

4 Everyone is ikcited.

[ ]

5 We're having a compitition.

[ ]

Read the text below. Choose the correct verb or verb group to correctly complete the sentences.

Swedish scientists ..... (6) ..... an experiment with fish. They fed the fish plastic glitter. They ..... (7) ..... that the fish got brain damage. They believe it ..... (8) ..... because of the glitter. I think it's cruel to experiment on animals like that.

6 A done B did C will do D do

7 A saying B asked C said D spoken

8 A are B got C were D was

9 Which word correctly completes the sentence?

.... a huge problem.

A it's
B its
C It's
D Its

10 Draw lines to connect the adjectives to the common nouns from the text.

black	children
excited	whale
dead	container
reusable	swan

11 Which conjunction can correctly join the clauses?

Plastic gets washed into the ocean .... animals eat it.

A so
B because
C and
D but

12 Which pronoun correctly completes the sentence?

'Tara and I won't use plastic,' said Flynn. .... teacher will be pleased.

A Her
B They
C Their
D Our

13 Which sentence is punctuated correctly?

A That's fantastic!.
B You're helping the environment
C Our teacher is Ms Dixon.
D We wont use plastic bottles.

14 Which sentence is punctuated correctly?

A who's the best?.
B whos turn is it?
C Whose lunch box is this?
D Who'se apple is this?

Answers and explanations on pages 113

What I did on the weekend

Last Friday evening I went with my family to the park. We went to buy street food for dinner and to listen to the band.

There were lots of different kinds of foods at the food stalls. We shared Vietnamese rice-paper rolls then I had pho. Pho is soup with noodles. It was delicious.

The band was good too. My sister is three. She loved the band. She danced energetically and bopped to the music. She was funny to watch. Mum took a video on her phone.

Mum liked it that the event had a Zero Waste Policy. All the food containers were made from bamboo and other natural organic materials so they were compostable. Nothing came in plastic and there were special recycling bins for all glass drink bottles. If you took your own water bottles you could refill them at the refilling stations. That's what we did. There was no litter and everything was recycled.

We had a great night.

By Ryan

1 The family had dinner

A in the park. B on the street. C at home.

2 What is pho? ....

3 The writer listened to the .... and watched his .... dance.

4 Mum took a video of

A the band. B Ryan's sister dancing. C Ryan eating dinner.

5 Circle the correct answer.

Could you buy water in plastic bottles at the event? Yes No

6 What do you think Ryan liked best about the event?

....

....

....

....

Answers and explanations on page 113

SPELLING

Write the correct spelling of the underlined words in questions 1–4.

1 There were diffrent foods.

2 The band played good musik.

3 We took refillable water bottels.

4 Mum took a video on her fone.

5 Write three words from the word family that includes **compostable**.

VOCABULARY

6 Circle the answer that has the nearest meaning to the underlined word.

Everything was recycled.

A regrown B reused
C repaired D reduced

7 Write a word from the text to match the meaning.

something that can be composted

8 There were lots of different food ....

9 Circle the word that does **not** belong.

A tasteless
B enjoyable
C delicious
D tasty

GRAMMAR

10 Complete the sentence with the correct article.

Ryan liked .... band

A the
B a
C an

11 Write a thinking verb to complete the sentence.

Mum .... the Zero Waste Policy.

12 Complete the sentence with an adverb that tells **how**.

My sister danced ....

13 Choose a conjunction to join the clauses correctly.

.... the band was still playing, we went home at 7 pm.

A Although
B Until
C Since
D Because

PUNCTUATION

Rewrite the sentences correctly.

14 thanks for taking us said ryan

15 I had fun said mum

Answers and explanations on page 113

What I did on the weekend

Last Friday evening I went with my family to the park. We went to buy street food for dinner and to listen to the band.

There were lots of different kinds of foods at the food stalls. We shared Vietnamese rice-paper rolls then I had pho. Pho is soup with noodles. It was delicious.

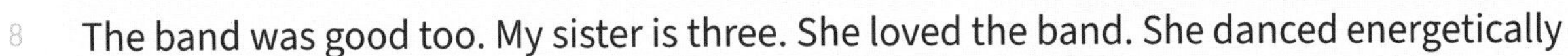

The band was good too. My sister is three. She loved the band. She danced energetically and bopped to the music. She was funny to watch. Mum took a video on her phone.

Mum liked it that the event had a Zero Waste Policy. All the food containers were made from bamboo and other natural organic materials so they were compostable. Nothing came in plastic and there were special recycling bins for all glass drink bottles. If you took your own water bottles you could refill them at the refilling stations. That's what we did. There was no litter and everything was recycled.

We had a great night.

By Ryan

1 The text

A describes Ryan and his family.

B tells about events that happened on Friday evening.

C gives information about an event that readers might like to attend.

2 The text is written from

A Mum's point of view.

B Ryan's sister's point of view.

C Ryan's point of view.

3 Link each paragraph to a statement.

Paragraph	Statement
1	A This is a summing-up of the text and a personal opinion.
2	B This is the introduction.
3	C This paragraph tells about the zero-waste policy.
4	D This paragraph tells about the food.
5	E This paragraph tells about the music.

4 Pho is a Vietnamese word. Link the words to their languages. You might need a dictionary.

Chinese Mexican Japanese Italian Greek

sushi moussaka pasta san choy bow tacos

5 The event was

A family friendly.

B just for adults.

C especially for children.

6 Based on information given by Ryan in the text, would you enjoy the event? Explain.

Get creative

7 What is your favourite food? Which country does it come from? Write a description. Include a photo.

Answers and explanations on page 113

Buried treasure

Characters: Calico Jack, Anne Bonny, Karl Starling, Mary Read
Setting: on board a pirate ship

Calico Jack: You all fought bravely. We have Spanish gold coins, rubies, diamonds, rice, sugar and bolts of cloth. We've paid the crew their share of the plunder and now we can share the rest of it. We'll keep the rice. The sugar and cloth we'll sell. What should we do with the gold and jewels?

Anne Bonny: Should we hide some of the loot, Captain?

Karl Starling (First Mate): Ay Jack, maybe we should hide some of it.

Mary Read: Where in the Caribbean would it be safe to hide such a bounty?

Anne Bonny: We'd need to bury it.

Karl Starling: We'd need to make a map so we remember where it is buried.

Calico Jack: I'd happily spend the gold and jewels. There's no need for a map or burying.

Mary Read: I agree. Let's spend it all in port and then find another ship to plunder.

Karl and Anne (together): Alright.

Calico Jack: It's a deal then.

1 What is the setting for the text? ....

....

2 The characters in the text are
A treasure hunters. B kings and queens. C pirates.

3 How did the characters get their treasure? ....

4 Why would they keep the rice? ....

5 What was the deal the four characters agreed to in the end?
A to spend the treasure B to bury the treasure C to make a map

6 Describe the life of the characters.

....

....

....

Answers and explanations on page 113

SPELLING

Write the correct spelling of the underlined words in questions 1–4.

1 Should we bury the treshure.

....

2 Berrying it is a good idea.

....

3 We'ill keep the rice.

....

4 How do we rememmber where we put it?

....

5 Write three words from the word family that includes **share**.

....

....

....

VOCABULARY

6 Circle the answer that has the nearest meaning to the underlined word.

Where will the treasure be safe?

A buried B kept

C secure D hidden

7 Write a word from the text to match the meaning.

a town or city with wharves for ships to dock ....

8 Add a word from the text to complete the sentence.

There were Spanish gold ....

9 Circle the word or word group that does **not** belong.

A loot B plunder

C money D stolen goods

GRAMMAR

10 Complete the sentence with the correct article.

'It's .... deal,' said Jack.

A the

B a

C an

11 Write a saying verb to complete the sentence.

'I am proud of each of you,' .... Jack.

12 Complete the sentence with an adverb that tells **how**.

You all fought ....

13 Choose a conjunction to correctly join the clauses.

.... I don't trust the mayor of the port, we'll keep our cargo secret from him.

A Although

B Until

C Since

D Because

PUNCTUATION

Rewrite the sentences correctly.

14 we should bury it said anne

....

....

....

15 I agree said mary

....

....

Answers and explanations on page 113

Buried treasure

Characters: Calico Jack, Anne Bonny, Karl Starling, Mary Read
Setting: on board a pirate ship

Calico Jack: You all fought bravely. We have Spanish gold coins, rubies, diamonds, rice, sugar and bolts of cloth. We've paid the crew their share of the plunder and now we can share the rest of it. We'll keep the rice. The sugar and cloth we'll sell. What should we do with the gold and jewels?

Anne Bonny: Should we hide some of the loot, Captain?

Karl Starling (First Mate): Ay Jack, maybe we should hide some of it.

Mary Read: Where in the Caribbean would it be safe to hide such a bounty?

Anne Bonny: We'd need to bury it.

Karl Starling: We'd need to make a map so we remember where it is buried.

Calico Jack: I'd happily spend the gold and jewels. There's no need for a map or burying.

Mary Read: I agree. Let's spend it all in port and then find another ship to plunder.

Karl and Anne (together): Alright.

Calico Jack: It's a deal then.

1 What kind of text is it?
A a conversation
B a play script
C a recount

2 What is the purpose of the text?
A to inform about treasure
B to entertain
C to recount true events

3 Calico Jack mentions paying the crew their share of the plunder. What is the plunder?

....

....

4 What does **it** refer to in the sentence below (lines 12–13)?
We'll need to make a map so we remember where it is buried.
A a map
B the loot
C the rice
D the gold coins

5 Who is the Captain?
A Anne Bonny
B Karl Starling
C Mary Read
D Calico Jack

6 How might olden-day pirates have remembered where they hid treasure?
A They made a map.
B They took a photo.
C They made a deal.

7 Write a story about hidden treasure.

Answers and explanations on page 113

READING AND COMPREHENSION

School Holiday Program

Hey Kids
Join us for our FREE fun-filled school holiday program.
Laugh, play, get active, make new friends and have fun.
Commencing 21 September for the school holidays

Featured fun activities include:

- Cycling circuits*
- Obstacle courses
- Skate and scooter sessions*
- Ninja warrior and Spartan team challenges
- Nature spy (limited places)
- Dance marathons
- Magician in training
- Pottery (limited places and fees apply)
- Karaoke (sing-a-long)
- Hula hoops, juggling, tug-o-war
- And much more.

There are fun activities to suit everyone.

*Bring your own equipment.
Equipment provided unless otherwise specified.

Full details of the program and further information

HERE

Note: Some activities require booking.

BOOK PROMPTLY

Program provided by Gold Coast City Council

1 Which organisation is running the holiday program?

....

....

2 Which activity would children join if they liked singing?

....

3 In which activities would you need to bring your own equipment?

....

....

4 What might 'Magician in training' involve?

....

....

....

5 Which activities require booking?

....

....

....

....

6 What does the photo show?

....

....

....

....

Answers and explanations on pages 113–114

SPELLING

Write the correct spelling of the underlined words in questions 1–4.

1 It's a school holiday programm.

....

2 The obstickle course sounds good.

....

3 Bring your own ekwipment.

....

4 I like team challunges.

....

5 Write three words from the word family that includes **available**.

....

....

....

VOCABULARY

6 Circle the answer that has the nearest meaning to the underlined word.
Some activities require booking.

A places
B reservation
C confirmation
D equipment

7 Write a word from the text to match the meaning.

people taking turns to sing along to a recording

....

8 Add a word or words from the text to complete the sentence.

....
apply for pottery.

9 Circle the word that does **not** belong.

A costs
B payment
C fees
D bounty

GRAMMAR

10 Complete the sentence with the correct article.

Full details of .... program can be found online.

A the
B a
C an

11 Write a relating (being) verb to complete the sentence.

There .... fun activities to interest everyone.

12 Complete the sentence with an adverb that tells **how**.

Some activities require booking.

Book ....

13 Choose a conjunction to correctly join the clauses.

The pottery program has been full .... it was first advertised.

A although
B until
C since
D because

PUNCTUATION

Rewrite the sentences correctly.

14 the program begins on 21 august

....

....

15 have a look at the gold coast city council website

....

....

Answers and explanations on page 114

TEXTS IN CONTEXT

School Holiday Program

Hey Kids
Join us for our FREE fun-filled school holiday program.
Laugh, play, get active, make new friends and have fun.
Commencing 21 September for the school holidays

Featured fun activities include:

- Cycling circuits*
- Obstacle courses
- Skate and scooter sessions*
- Ninja warrior and Spartan team challenges
- Nature spy (limited places)
- Dance marathons
- Magician in training
- Pottery (limited places and fees apply)
- Karaoke (sing-a-long)
- Hula hoops, juggling, tug-o-war
- And much more.

There are fun activities to suit everyone.

*Bring your own equipment.
Equipment provided unless otherwise specified.

Full details of the program and further information

HERE

Note: Some activities require booking.

BOOK PROMPTLY

Program provided by Gold Coast City Council

1 The text is
- **A** an advertisement.
- **B** an information report.
- **C** a newspaper article.

2 The text is written for
- **A** children.
- **B** adults.
- **C** teachers.

3 Choose **all** that apply. The text includes
- **A** a list of activities.
- **B** commands.
- **C** explanations.
- **D** a date.
- **E** a link for extra information

4 The text repeats the word **fun** to emphasise it. Circle the word in the text. How many times is it used?

5 Which activities are not listed that you think should be included in the program?

....

....

....

6 Do you think the poster will get children to join the school holiday program? Explain.

....

....

....

....

7 Choose **two** of the advertised activities that you would like to do. Give reasons for your choices.

Answers and explanations on page 114

READING AND COMPREHENSION

My favourite place

When Roshni and I stay at Dad's place for the weekend, he takes us to the Royal National Park. We love to go bushwalking.

We love walking through the rainforest, past the tall eucalypts, the casuarina trees and the cabbage tree palms. In summer the flowers on the cabbage tree palms look like cabbages. Dad loves the Gymea lilies best. They have big red flowers on giant stems. They can grow up to four metres high. They flower in the winter.

Dad carries a backpack with our supplies and we have a leisurely picnic lunch at Bola Creek picnic area. It's very quiet and peaceful there. We listen to the different birds and the water trickling in the creek as we eat. It's quite close to the city but you'd think we were a million kilometres from it.

The Royal National Park is my favourite place in the world. Dad says it's probably his too.

By Tami, age 7 and a half

1. Where is Tami's favourite place? ....

2. What colour are Gymea lilies? ....

3. What is the main reason Tami goes to the National Park?
   A to eat lunch **B** to see the trees **C** to go bushwalking

4. List the plants Tami sees in her favourite place. ....

5. List the things Tami hears in her favourite place. ....

6. How would Dad feel if he read this text? ....

Answers and explanations on page 114

SPELLING

Write the correct spelling of the underlined words in questions 1–4.

1 The flowers look like cabbiges.

....

2 It's peacful in the park.

....

3 The city seems a million kilometars away.

....

4 The park is Tami's favourite place in the werld.

....

5 Write three words from the word family that includes **supplies**.

....

....

....

VOCABULARY

6 Circle the answer that has the nearest meaning to the underlined word.

Gymea lilies have giant stems.

A skinny
B large
C strong
D amazing

7 Write a word or word group from the text to match the meaning.

a place filled with trees and plants

....

8 Add a word or words from the text to complete the sentence.

The park is .... close to the city.

9 Circle the word that does **not** belong.

A stream
B river
C creek
D ocean

GRAMMAR

10 Complete the sentence with the correct article.

He takes us to .... Royal National Park.

A the
B a
C an

11 Write a relating (being) verb to complete the sentence.

Gymea lilies .... big red flowers.

12 Complete the sentence with an adverb that tells **how**.

They eat a .... lunch.

13 Choose a conjunction to correctly join the clauses.

.... it's so quiet, we can hear all the different birds.

A Although
B Until
C As
D Because

PUNCTUATION

Rewrite the sentences correctly.

14 we go hiking in the royal national park

....

....

15 dad roshni and tami have lunch at bola creek

....

....

Answers and explanations on page 114

My favourite place

When Roshni and I stay at Dad's place for the weekend, he takes us to the Royal National Park. We love to go bushwalking.

We love walking through the rainforest, past the tall eucalypts, the casuarina trees and the cabbage tree palms. In summer the flowers on the cabbage tree palms look like cabbages. Dad loves the Gymea lilies best. They have big red flowers on giant stems. They can grow up to four metres high. They flower in the winter.

Dad carries a backpack with our supplies and we have a leisurely picnic lunch at Bola Creek picnic area. It's very quiet and peaceful there. We listen to the different birds and the water trickling in the creek as we eat. It's quite close to the city but you'd think we were a million kilometres from it.

The Royal National Park is my favourite place in the world. Dad says it's probably his too.

By Tami, age 7 and a half

1 The purpose of the text is to
- **A** share an opinion about a place.
- **B** persuade others to visit a place.
- **C** persuade others to love the Royal National Park.

2 The writer
- **A** had to research the topic to write her text.
- **B** writes knowledgeably about her topic.
- **C** does not know a great deal about her topic.

3 Link each paragraph to a statement.

Paragraph	Statement
1	**A** This paragraph tells about the plants and trees.
2	**B** This paragraph is the summing-up statement.
3	**C** This paragraph introduces the topic.
4	**D** This paragraph tells about the picnic area.

4 The text includes terminology related to trees and plants. Write the specific terms.

5 Tami writes that 'It's quite close to the city but you'd think we were a million kilometres from it' (lines 11–12). Explain what she means.

....

....

6 Does the text inspire you to

A	go hiking?	Yes	No
B	visit a National Park?	Yes	No
C	get outdoors to appreciate the trees and flowers?	Yes	No
D	exercise more?	Yes	No
E	think about your favourite place?	Yes	No

7 Write a description of one of your favourite places. Give reasons why it's a favourite.

Answers and explanations on page 114

READING AND COMPREHENSION

Training Band

COME JOIN OUR BAND!

We meet 8 am Tuesdays and Thursdays in the assembly hall.
Choose from baritone horn, bass clarinet, bass guitar, clarinet, euphonium, flute, percussion, saxophone, trombone or trumpet.

Learning a musical instrument helps with memory, maths, learning other languages and coordination.

Joining the band will give you a sense of achievement and increased confidence.

You will overcome stage fright.

We build teamwork and friendship.

We'd love you to join us.

No musical experience required. We will teach you.

You will steadily improve.

Just bring yourself along.

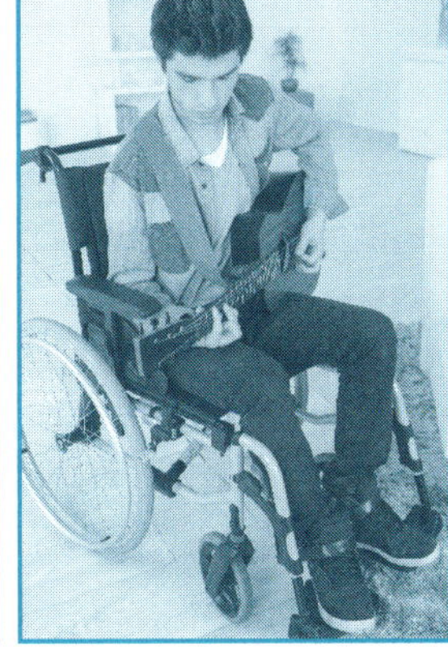

1 Which of the following instruments can you learn in the school band? Choose **all** that apply.

- **A** bagpipes
- **B** bass guitar
- **C** tuba
- **D** harp
- **E** trombone

2 Choose **all** that apply. The text says that learning a musical instrument helps with

- **A** learning another language.
- **B** doing maths.
- **C** concentration.
- **D** developing confidence.
- **E** playing sport.
- **F** improving memory.
- **G** doing your homework.

3 'Stage fright' (line 14) means

- **A** being frightened of a stage.
- **B** being frightened to perform for an audience.
- **C** getting a fright from an audience.

4 How can joining the band help you overcome stage fright?

....

....

5 How can joining the band help build teamwork and friendship?

....

....

6 Does the text make you want to join this band? Explain.

....

....

....

Answers and explanations on page 114

SPELLING

Write the correct spelling of the underlined words in questions 1–4.

1 Meet in the assembully hall.

2 Learn a musickle instrument.

3 You'll get a sense of acheevment.

4 It helps you learn another langwige.

5 Write three words from the word family that includes **choose**.

VOCABULARY

6 Circle the answer that has the nearest meaning to the underlined word.

You'll have increased confidence.

A useful **B** amazing
C improved **D** bigger

7 Write a word from the text to match the meaning.

musical instruments that you play by banging, shaking or striking

8 Add a word from the text to complete the sentence.

No musical .... required.

9 Circle the word that does **not** belong.

A trumpet **B** trombone
C percussion **D** saxophone

GRAMMAR

10 Complete the sentence with the correct article.

Get .... sense of achievement.

A the
B a
C an

11 Write a relating (being) verb to complete the sentence.

'The Royal National Park .... my favourite place,' announced Tami.

12 Complete the sentence with an adverb that tells **how**.

You will .... improve.

13 Choose a conjunction to correctly join the clauses.

.... you've given it a go, you won't know if you like it or not.

A Although
B Until
C Since
D Because

PUNCTUATION

Rewrite the sentences correctly.

14 we meet tuesdays and thursdays

15 choose from clarinet euphonium flute percussion saxophone trombone or trumpet

Answers and explanations on pages 114–115

TEXTS IN CONTEXT

Training Band

COME JOIN OUR BAND!

We meet 8 am Tuesdays and Thursdays in the assembly hall. Choose from baritone horn, bass clarinet, bass guitar, clarinet, euphonium, flute, percussion, saxophone, trombone or trumpet.

Learning a musical instrument helps with memory, maths, learning other languages and coordination.

Joining the band will give you a sense of achievement and increased confidence.

You will overcome stage fright.

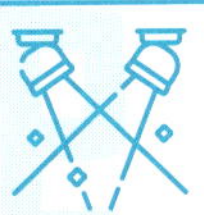

We build teamwork and friendship.

We'd love you to join us.

No musical experience required. We will teach you.

You will steadily improve.

Just bring yourself along.

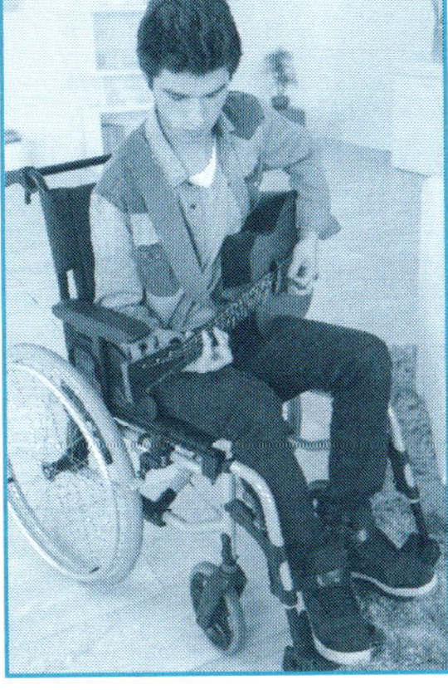

1. The purpose of the text is to
   - A tell people when the school band performs.
   - B encourage children to join the school band.
   - C tell people about the school band.

2. The audience for the text is
   - A parents at the school.
   - B anyone at the school.
   - C children at the school.

3. Choose **all** that apply. The text
   - A lists reasons for joining the band.
   - B tells when the band meets.
   - C tells which instruments you'll need to bring.
   - D tells where the band meets.
   - E tells the name of the band teachers.
   - F tells who is the organiser of the band.

4. Are the images in the text effective? Explain.

   ....

   ....

   ....

5. Choose **all** that apply. The text
   - A makes it seem difficult to join the band.
   - B makes it seem easy to join the band.
   - C tells you that you will be welcome in the band.

6. What do the photos show you about the band?

   ....

   ....

   ....

Get creative

7. Create a poster that tells about something that's happening in your class or school.

Answers and explanations on page 115

What I learned in sport this year

Tara: I play soccer and I love it. The most important thing I learnt this year at soccer was how to be a good loser. That's what being a good sport is all about. My team lost more games than we won and some of the players got really disappointed with the team. Our coach said the most important thing to remember when playing sport is to have fun.

We learnt that trying our hardest and always doing our best makes us winners, whether we win the game or not.

We learnt to thank the other team for their game. We thank our coach for her support. We congratulate each other on doing our best. We agree that having fun is the best thing about playing soccer.

Simon: I like swimming. I learnt that I don't enjoy competitions. I like individual sports where I can do my best and not worry about disappointing others or letting the team down. I don't like feeling that I am to blame if the team loses. I am good at swimming but I don't swim quickly. I don't swim in races. I just enjoy swimming.

1 What sport does Tara play? ....

2 What did Simon learn this year in sport?

A that he doesn't like competing **B** that he's good at swimming **C** that he likes swimming

3 Tara says the best thing about soccer is

A winning games.
B having fun.
C thanking the other team for the game.

4 Tara says that to be a good sport you have to be

A a winner. **B** great at your game. **C** a good loser.

5 Why do you thank a coach? ....

....

....

6 What is Tara's definition of a winner?

....

....

Answers and explanations on page 115

SPELLING

Write the correct spelling of the underlined words in questions 1–4.

1 I like individuel sports.

2 We like competitians.

3 It's dissapointing when you lose.

4 Congrachulate the winners.

5 Write three words from the word family that includes **coach**.

VOCABULARY

6 Circle the answer that has the nearest meaning to the underlined word.

We applaud the other team's victory.

A support B win
C loss D draw

7 Write a word from the text to match the meaning.

to say or feel that someone is responsible for a loss or a problem

8 Add a word from the text to complete the sentence.

A good ______ knows how to be a good loser.

9 Circle the word that does **not** belong.

A learn B train
C coach D instruct

GRAMMAR

10 Complete the sentence with the correct article.

Learn how to be ______ good loser.

A the
B a
C an

11 Write a thinking verb to complete the sentence.

It's important to ______ that we play sport for fun.

12 Complete the sentence with an adverb that tells **how**.

Simon doesn't swim ______.

13 Choose a conjunction to correctly join the clauses.

______ we know how to be good losers, we prefer to win.

A Although
B Until
C Since
D Because

PUNCTUATION

Rewrite the sentences correctly.

14 I dont like team sport said simon

15 ms chen is our soccer coach said tara

Answers and explanations on page 115

What I learned in sport this year

Tara: I play soccer and I love it. The most important thing I learnt this year at soccer was how to be a good loser. That's what being a good sport is all about. My team lost more games than we won and some of the players got really disappointed with the team. Our coach said the most important thing to remember when playing sport is to have fun.

We learnt that trying our hardest and always doing our best makes us winners, whether we win the game or not.

We learnt to thank the other team for their game. We thank our coach for her support. We congratulate each other on doing our best. We agree that having fun is the best thing about playing soccer.

Simon: I like swimming. I learnt that I don't enjoy competitions. I like individual sports where I can do my best and not worry about disappointing others or letting the team down. I don't like feeling that I am to blame if the team loses. I am good at swimming but I don't swim quickly. I don't swim in races. I just enjoy swimming.

1 The purpose of each child's text is to
- A describe a sport.
- B present an opinion.
- C persuade others to play a sport they like.

2 Tara and Simon have written texts to
- A help them decide which sport to play next year.
- B reflect on their year of sport.
- C reflect on the types of sport available to them.

3 Each child's text structure consists of
- A an orientation to the sport, a description of the sport and a personal opinion.
- B an introduction, the rules of the sport and reasons to like the sport.
- C a statement of opinion, supporting reasons and a summing up.

4 Tara uses the pronouns *I* and *we*. Simon uses *I* and not *we*. Why is there a difference?

....

....

5 Have Simon and Tara each adequately explained themselves? Can you understand their reasoning? Explain.

....

....

....

6 Which child's opinion do you agree with most? Explain.

....

....

....

7 What kinds of sport do you enjoy most? Write your reasons.

Answers and explanations on page 115

Thank a tree

It's important to appreciate trees.

Every day you should hug a tree and say, 'Thank you, sincerely, for being here.'

Why?

Because:

- Trees make the oxygen that all animals need to breathe.
- Trees take in the carbon dioxide that all animals breathe out and that is made in cars and factories.
- Tree roots hold soil in place.
- Trees provide homes for birds, possums, koalas, insects, lizards and other creatures.
- Trees provide food for animals.
- Trees give shade from the sun and block the wind.
- In cities and towns trees buffer our homes from traffic noise.
- Trees are beautiful.

Showing appreciation and gratitude

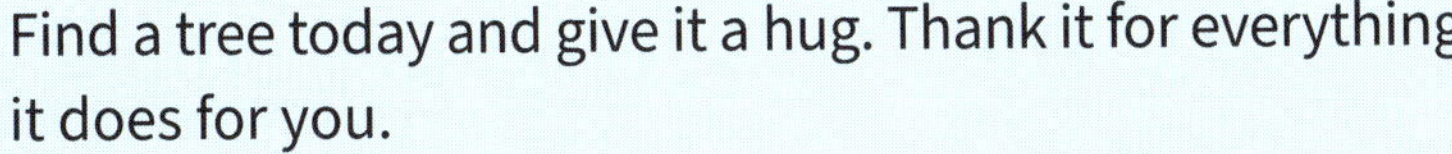

Find a tree today and give it a hug. Thank it for everything it does for you.

1. List **two** ways in which humans make carbon dioxide.

   ....

2. What do all animals need to breathe?

   ....

3. Which parts of trees are food for animals? Choose **all** that apply.

   A leaves **B** flowers **C** seeds

4. What could happen to soil if there were no tree roots?

   ....

5. What is the most important thing a tree does?

   ....

6. Do you think humans value trees enough or do we mostly just take trees for granted? Explain your answer.

   ....

   ....

Answers and explanations on page 115

SPELLING

Write the correct spelling of the underlined words in questions 1–4.

1 Trees are beutiful.

2 Trees make life possable.

3 Trees breathe carbin dioxide.

4 Possoms nest in trees.

5 Write three words from the word family that includes **shade**.

VOCABULARY

6 Circle the answer that has the nearest meaning to the underlined word.

Cars make carbon dioxide.

A expel B produce
C emit D use

7 Write a word from the text to match the meaning.

a barrier against something unwanted, such as traffic noise ....

8 Add a word from the text to complete the sentence.

Trees make .... so animals can breathe.

9 Circle the word that does **not** belong.

A gratitude B thanks
C appreciation D ingratitude

GRAMMAR

10 Complete the sentence with the correct article.

Hug .... tree today.

A the
B a
C an

11 Write an auxilliary (helping) verb to complete the sentence.

'I .... trying as hard as I can,' said Dua.

12 Complete the sentence with an adverb that tells **how**.

We .... thank you, trees.

13 Choose a conjunction to correctly join the clauses.

.... trees are vital for our survival, we need to look after them.

A Although
B Until
C Therefore
D Because

PUNCTUATION

Rewrite the sentences correctly.

14 thank you for being here said josef

15 I love trees said chanel

Answers and explanations on page 115

Thank a tree

It's important to appreciate trees.

Every day you should hug a tree and say, 'Thank you, sincerely, for being here.'

Why?

Because:

- Trees make the oxygen that all animals need to breathe.
- Trees take in the carbon dioxide that all animals breathe out and that is made in cars and factories.
- Tree roots hold soil in place.
- Trees provide homes for birds, possums, koalas, insects, lizards and other creatures.
- Trees provide food for animals.
- Trees give shade from the sun and block the wind.
- In cities and towns trees buffer our homes from traffic noise.
- Trees are beautiful.

Find a tree today and give it a hug. Thank it for everything it does for you.

Showing appreciation and gratitude

1 The purpose of the text is to
- **A** entertain readers with ideas about trees.
- **B** persuade readers to take action.
- **C** provide scientific evidence that trees help people breathe.

2 The text was written for
- **A** children.
- **B** scientists.
- **C** a television audience.

3 Link each part of the text to a statement of purpose.

1 The heading	**A** This illustrates something in the text.
2 The opening statement	**B** This gives a clue to what the text is about.
3 The list of reasons	**C** This introduces the writer's position on the topic.
4 The closing statement	**D** This supports the opening statement.
5 The photo	**E** This sums up and reinforces the opening statement.

4 The photo shows someone
- **A** playing a game in a park.
- **B** saying thank you to a tree.
- **C** protecting a tree.

5 Does the text make you want to find a tree to hug? Explain.

....

....

6 Aside from saying thank you, what else can people do to show they value trees?

....

....

7 Write a poem about a tree or make a poster to encourage people to value trees.

Answers and explanations on pages 115–116

READING AND COMPREHENSION

Tornado hits Bundaberg

Newsreader: A tornado hit Bundaberg in the early hours of this morning. Bundaberg resident Zara Inam was interviewed outside the rubble that was once her home. She says she survived by hiding in her bathroom with her partner and their cat. They lay fearfully in the bathtub with a mattress pulled over the top of them.

Zara: It was terrifying. The wind roared. It was deafening. There was crashing and banging. The tornado only lasted a few minutes but it seemed like an hour. I wondered if we'd make it out.

Newsreader: A tornado is a powerful column of wind from a thunderstorm. The wind in the column moves in a spiral. Tornadoes are also called twisters. They can be very destructive. Emergency services are helping people in Bundaberg clear up the mess from fallen trees and power lines.

In other news today …

A Bundaberg house in ruins after a tornado strike

1 Where did the tornado strike? ....

2 Where did Zara hide? ....

....

3 What had been damaged by the tornado? Choose **all** that apply.

A houses B trees C powerlines D emergency services

4 Why is a tornado also called a twister?

....

....

5 What sounds did Zara hear? Choose **all** that apply.

A crashing B banging C the wind roaring

6 Why would 'a few minutes' have 'seemed like an hour' (line 7)? Explain.

....

....

....

Answers and explanations on page 116

SPELLING

Write the correct spelling of the underlined words in questions 1–4.

1 Tornadohs can be destructive.

2 It's a powerful columm of wind.

3 Emergincy services were called.

4 She servived in her bathroom.

5 Write three words from the word family that includes **terrifying**.

VOCABULARY

6 Circle the answer that has the nearest meaning to the underlined word.

Residents need to clear up the mess.

A pollution B debris
C trees D houses

7 Write a word from the text to match the meaning.

when a noise is so loud you can't hear anything else

8 Add a word from the text to complete the sentence.

A tornado is a column of wind from a ________.

9 Circle the word that does **not** belong.

A roared B screamed
C shrieked D murmured

GRAMMAR

10 Complete the sentence with the correct noun group.

A tornado is ________.

11 Write an auxilliary (helping) verb to complete the sentence.

Emergency services ________ help all residents as soon as possible.

12 Complete the sentence with an adverb that tells **how**.

They lay ________ in the bathtub.

13 Choose a conjunction to correctly join the clauses.

A Although
B Until
C Since
D Because

________ tornadoes do occur in Australia, they are not as common here as in America.

PUNCTUATION

Rewrite the sentences correctly.

14 we were terrified declared zara

15 how is your house asked chris

Answers and explanations on page 116

Tornado hits Bundaberg

Newsreader: A tornado hit Bundaberg in the early hours of this morning. Bundaberg resident Zara Inam was interviewed outside the rubble that was once her home. She says she survived by hiding in her bathroom with her partner and their cat. They lay fearfully in the bathtub with a mattress pulled over the top of them.

Zara: It was terrifying. The wind roared. It was deafening. There was crashing and banging. The tornado only lasted a few minutes but it seemed like an hour. I wondered if we'd make it out.

Newsreader: A tornado is a powerful column of wind from a thunderstorm. The wind in the column moves in a spiral. Tornadoes are also called twisters. They can be very destructive. Emergency services are helping people in Bundaberg clear up the mess from fallen trees and power lines.

In other news today …

A Bundaberg house in ruins after a tornado strike

1 The purpose of the text is to
- A warn about tornadoes.
- B give advice about what to do in case of a tornado.
- C inform about a tornado event.

2 The audience for the text is
- A children.
- B teachers and children in classrooms.
- C television viewers.

3 Choose **all** that apply. The text includes
- A a definition of a tornado.
- B an interview.
- C a newsworthy photo.
- D information about a newsworthy event.
- E a story about a cat.
- F other news items.

4 Which words in the text help you understand why Zara was frightened? Write **four**.

....

....

5 How interesting was the text for you? Circle a rating where 1 is not interesting at all and 5 is very interesting.

1 2 3 4 5

6 Explain the rating you gave the text and your reasons.

....

....

....

....

Get creative

7 Write a news report about a newsworthy event at your school. Film a classmate reading the report for a TV news program.

Answers and explanations on page 116

An Elder

This is Yia Yia. She is my mother's grandmother. She always does most of the cooking and planning when we have a family celebration. She can cook for a crowd of 40 people—no problem. I especially love her spanakopitakia (mini spinach pies with fetta cheese).

Every year Yia Yia makes a St Basil's cake (vasilopita) for New Year's Day. St Basil is the Santa Claus of Greece. He brings gifts on the first night of the new year. A St Basil's cake has a coin inside it. Yia Yia slices the cake and hands it out to family members from the oldest to the youngest, in order. If you find the coin in your piece of cake you will have a lucky year. Everyone hopes to find the coin.

Yia Yia is a strong woman and a respected family member. She is also kind and loving and everyone adores her. She loves Greek music and does all the Greek folk dances. She has taught me a lot of things.

1 Who gets the last slice of St Basil's cake?
- A the oldest person
- B the youngest person
- C Yia Yia
- D St Basil

2 Name **two** ingredients used in spanakopitakia.

3 The photo shows
- A Yia Yia's great grandmother.
- B the writer.
- C the writer's great grandmother.
- D Yia Yia's mother.

4 Choose **all** that apply. Yia Yia is valued for her
- A strength of character.
- B strong muscles.
- C cooking.
- D kindness.

5 How does the writer feel about Yia Yia?
- A respectful and loving
- B patient and loving
- C impatient but respectful
- D grateful but bored

6 Choose **all** that apply. Everyone wants a piece of the St Basil's cake because
- A it's delicious.
- B Yia Yia bakes it.
- C they want to get the lucky coin.
- D it's served at family gatherings.

7 Choose **all** that apply. What is Yia Yia likely to have taught family members?
- A cooking
- B folk dancing
- C kite flying
- D to value family
- E to value cultural traditions
- F to appreciate Greek music

Answers and explanations on page 116

Each sentence has one word that is incorrect. Write the correct spelling of the underlined word in the box.

1 Yia Yia dose most of the cooking.

2 Yia Yia is good at planing.

3 The pies are espeshly popular.

4 The yungest family members love the cake too.

5 Yia Yia is loveing.

Read the text below. Choose the correct verb or verb group to complete the sentences.

> Yia Yia ___(6)___ cook for a large crowd. She always cooks the St Basil's cake. The cake ___(7)___ a gold coin in it. If you get the coin you ___(8)___ a lucky year.

6 A done B did C can D do

7 A was B are C is D has

8 A have B will have C did have D are having

9 Choose the correct article to complete the sentence.

The St Basil's cake contains a gold coin. Everyone wants to find ______ coin.

A a
B an
C the

10 Which thinking verb correctly completes the sentence?

Everyone ______ Yia Yia.

A adore
B adoring
C adores
D were adoring

11 Which conjunction correctly joins the clauses?

______ Yia Yia bakes a great cake I prefer her spanakopitakia.

A Although B Until
C Since D Because

12 Which pronoun correctly completes the sentence?

If ______ get the coin you will have a lucky year.

A her B they
C you D we

13 Which sentence is punctuated correctly?
A 'I love these pies! Said George.'
B 'Me too?' said Mark.
C 'May I have a pie?' asked Juno.
D 'Of course,' replied Yia Yia

14 Which sentence is punctuated correctly?
A don't eat all the cake!
B Don't eat the coin!
C Wholl get the coin?
D I want the coin?

Answers and explanations on page 116

READING AND COMPREHENSION

CARS AND VEHICLES | HOME AND GARDEN | SPORT AND ADVENTURE | CLOTHING AND JEWELLERY

For sale

Two-person tent $79

- Strong and waterproof
- Easy to put up
- Heavy-duty floor to keep you dry
- Zipped front opening with Velcro storm flaps to keep the wind out
- Private—no windows
- Fibreglass poles
- Mesh panels inside for storage
- Only used a few times. Well looked-after. Looks as new.
- Brisbane area
- Contact Pratika: pratika18@hotmail.com

Two-person tent
$120 or make an offer

- Ultra-lightweight—perfect for hiking
- Automatic pop-up—no trouble to put up
- Waterproof, stormproof and insect-proof
- Orange polyester
- Almost new
- Location—Brisbane
- Contact Emil: emilos22@gmail.com

1 Where would you need to go to collect both tents? ....

2 Both tents are

A new. B second-hand. C unused.

3 Which tent would be the lightest to carry? Explain.

....

4 Which tent would be the sturdiest? Explain.

....

5 Which tent would be the easiest to put up? Explain.

....

6 Which **two** features do you think would be the most important in a tent?

....

....

Answers and explanations on page 116

SPELLING

Write the correct spelling of the underlined words in questions 1–4.

1 Hevy-duty floors keep you dry.

....

2 The tent has no windows so is privite.

....

3 The tent is waterprewf.

....

4 It is lightwait.

....

5 Write three words from the word family that includes **storage**.

....

....

VOCABULARY

6 Circle the answer that has the nearest meaning to the underlined words.

It's no trouble to put up.

A difficult B easy
C complicated D possible

7 Write a word from the text to match the meaning.

done instantly and quickly without thought

....

8 Add a word from the text to complete the sentence.

The tent has mesh panels for

....

9 Circle the word that does **not** belong.

A perfect B exceptional
C flawed D ideal

GRAMMAR

10 Complete the sentence with a noun group.

The zipped front opening has

....

11 Write a verb group to complete the sentence.

The $79 tent .... a few times.

12 Complete the sentence with an adverb or prepositional phrase that tells **where**, **when** or **how**.

The storm flaps keep the wind

....

13 Add a conjunction to correctly join the clauses.

It's lightweight ....
it's perfect for hiking.

PUNCTUATION

Rewrite the sentences correctly.

14 contact pratika in brisbane to buy the $79 tent

....

....

....

....

15 i prefer the orange tent said elizabeth

....

....

....

Answers and explanations on page 116

CARS AND VEHICLES | HOME AND GARDEN | **SPORT AND ADVENTURE** | CLOTHING AND JEWELLERY

For sale

Two-person tent $79

- Strong and waterproof
- Easy to put up
- Heavy-duty floor to keep you dry
- Zipped front opening with Velcro storm flaps to keep the wind out
- Private—no windows
- Fibreglass poles
- Mesh panels inside for storage
- Only used a few times. Well looked-after. Looks as new.
- Brisbane area
- Contact Pratika: pratika18@hotmail.com

Two-person tent
$120 or make an offer

- Ultra-lightweight—perfect for hiking
- Automatic pop-up—no trouble to put up
- Waterproof, stormproof and insect-proof
- Orange polyester
- Almost new
- Location—Brisbane
- Contact Emil: emilos22@gmail.com

1 The texts are
 A newspaper advertisements.
 B internet advertisements.
 C television advertisements.

2 The audience for the texts is
 A children.
 B hikers.
 C anyone who wants to buy a tent.

3 Choose **all** that apply. The advertisements include
 A how to contact the sellers.
 B product prices.
 C important features of the products.
 D explanations of what you would use the products for.
 E descriptions of the sellers.
 F information about other buyers.

4 Which photo is more useful to buyers? Explain. 

5 Why might the sellers be selling their tents?
 A They don't use them anymore.
 B They have holes in them.
 C They are worn out.

6 Which of the two tents would you choose to buy and why?

....

....

....

7 Create an advertisement to sell something that you no longer want or something imaginary. 

Answers and explanations on page 117

The whale shark

What it looks like

A whale shark is a giant fish. It's the biggest fish in the ocean. It can grow as long as a school bus. The only animal in the world that is bigger than a whale shark is a whale. A whale shark is grey-brown with a white belly and pale yellow spots and stripes. It can live for 100 years.

Where it lives

The whale shark likes warm topical waters. It swims long distances during migration.

What it eats

A whale shark has rows of tiny teeth but they aren't used for eating. It is a filter feeder. It opens its mouth to scoop up water with plankton (tiny plants as well as tiny animals such as krill, fish eggs and crab larvae), then it filters out the water like a sieve to expel it and keep the food.

Its status

Whale sharks are a threatened species. They are protected under international law but they are still hunted in China, and other places in Asia, for their meat and fins (for shark-fin soup). Some are kept in aquariums in Japan, the USA and China although animal welfare groups object to this.

1 A whale shark is a

A whale. B fish. C sea mammal.

2 Choose **all** that apply. Whale sharks are kept in aquariums in

A Australia. B the USA. C China. D Japan.

3 A 'threatened species' (line 13) is one which is

A under threat of extinction. B a threat to other species. C threatened by predators.

4 Why might people break the law and kill whale sharks? Choose **all** that apply.

A They don't care about the law.
B They can make money selling whale-shark meat.
C They don't know about the law.

5 What should happen to people who sell or buy whale-shark meat?

....

6 How do you think a whale shark would feel about living in an aquarium?

....

....

Answers and explanations on page 117

SPELLING

Write the correct spelling of the underlined words in questions 1–4.

1 It's the biggest fish in the oshen.

2 The wail shark is grey-brown.

3 Intanational law protects the sharks.

4 They scoop up plangtin.

5 Write three words from the word family that includes **hunted**.

VOCABULARY

6 Circle the answer that has the nearest meaning to the underlined word.

There are laws to protect the sharks.

A traditions　　B rules
C practices　　D habits

7 Write a word from the text to match the meaning.

searched for or tracked down

8 Add a word from the text to complete the sentence.

A whale shark is a ______ feeder.

9 Circle the word that does **not** belong.

A expel　　B swallow
C remove　　D eject

GRAMMAR

10 Complete the sentence with a noun group.

A whale shark can grow as long as ______.

11 Write a verb group to complete the sentence.

The whale shark's teeth ______ for eating.

12 Complete the sentence with an adverb or prepositional phrase that tells **where**, **when** or **how**.

They swim long distances ______.

13 Add a conjunction to correctly join the clauses.

______ they are protected, they are still hunted.

PUNCTUATION

Rewrite the sentences correctly.

14 some are kept in aquariums in japan the usa and china

15 i feel sad for whale sharks in fish tanks said jed

Answers and explanations on page 117

The whale shark

What it looks like

A whale shark is a giant fish. It's the biggest fish in the ocean. It can grow as long as a school bus. The only animal in the world that is bigger than a whale shark is a whale. A whale shark is grey-brown with a white belly and pale yellow spots and stripes. It can live for 100 years.

Where it lives

The whale shark likes warm topical waters. It swims long distances during migration.

What it eats

A whale shark has rows of tiny teeth but they aren't used for eating. It is a filter feeder. It opens its mouth to scoop up water with plankton (tiny plants as well as tiny animals such as krill, fish eggs and crab larvae), then it filters out the water like a sieve to expel it and keep the food.

Its status

Whale sharks are a threatened species. They are protected under international law but they are still hunted in China, and other places in Asia, for their meat and fins (for shark-fin soup). Some are kept in aquariums in Japan, the USA and China although animal welfare groups object to this.

1 The text is

- **A** an information report.
- **B** a story.
- **C** a news report.

2 The writer of the text

- **A** is not well informed about whale sharks.
- **B** writes in a way that is easy to understand.
- **C** uses technical terms that do not suit the text.

3 Circle true or false after each statement.

Whale sharks

A	have big, sharp teeth.	True	False
B	migrate.	True	False
C	eat plankton.	True	False
D	chew their food.	True	False
E	like warm, tropical water.	True	False
F	have grey spots on their bellies.	True	False

4 Choose **all** that apply. The text includes

- **A** a heading.
- **B** subheadings.
- **C** paragraphs.
- **D** a conclusion.
- **E** a command.
- **F** statements.
- **G** opinions.

5 Under which new subheading would you find this information?

Females give birth to live young.

- **A** Where it breeds
- **B** Its habitat
- **C** How it breeds

6 The layout of the text

- **A** is not very useful.
- **B** helps readers find specific information.
- **C** makes it harder for readers to find specific information.

7 Research an animal and write a report.

Answers and explanations on page 117

An odd-looking creature

The platypus is an odd-looking creature. It's a furry mammal but it has a bill like a duck and webbed feet. It doesn't have teeth. The platypus paddles with its front feet and steers with its back feet and tail. Its nostrils close underwater. The platypus uses its bill to sense where it is going. Males have venomous heel spurs on their back feet.

A platypus eats insects, worms, shellfish and larvae. It uses its bill to scoop food, along with mud and small rocks, from the bottom of ponds. Because it doesn't have teeth, the platypus uses the rocks to grind the food in its bill into smaller bits.

A female lays one or two eggs in a burrow. She keeps her eggs warm by holding them between her body and her tail. Babies can swim on their own when they are about three or four months old.

The platypus only lives along the east coast of Australia. Its future is uncertain because the places where it lives are being destroyed to build houses for people. Some platypuses also get caught and drown in yabby traps that people leave in creeks and rivers.

A platypus with a worm

1 A platypus is a

A type of duck.
B mammal.
C sea mammal.

2 Choose **all** that apply. All platypuses have

A teeth.
B paddles.
C webbed feet.
D fur.
E spurs.
F bills.

3 To eat, the platypus

A chews food.
B pulls food apart with its spurs.
C grinds food with rocks.

4 Its webbed feet help the platypus

A walk on land.
B swim in the water.
C dig tunnels.

5 The platypus

A has live babies like dogs and cats.
B lays eggs like birds and most reptiles.
C breathes underwater like a fish.

6 What is the biggest threat to platypuses? ....

....

Answers and explanations on page 117

SPELLING

Write the correct spelling of the underlined words in questions 1–4.

1 The platapuss is odd-looking.

....

2 Mails have spurs.

....

3 The spurs are venimus.

....

4 Platypuses get court in yabby traps.

....

5 Write three words from the word family that includes **cover**.

....

....

VOCABULARY

6 Circle the answer that has the nearest meaning to the underlined words.

The platypus paddles with its front feet.

A propels B steers
C pokes D pushes

7 Write a word from the text to match the meaning.

something that is toxic and can poison or kill you

....

8 Add a word from the text to complete the sentence.

Its .... close underwater.

9 Circle the word that does **not** belong.

A pond B burrow
C stream D creek

GRAMMAR

10 Complete the sentence with a noun group.

It uses its .... to steer.

11 Write a verb group to complete the sentence.

Places where the platypus lives

.... for people's housing.

12 Complete the sentence with an adverb or prepositional phrase that tells **where**, **when** or **how**.

The platypus only lives ....

....

13 Add a conjunction to correctly join the clauses.

The platypus has nowhere to live

.... of land clearing.

PUNCTUATION

Rewrite the sentences correctly.

14 it scoops insects worms mud small rocks shellfish and larvae into its bill

....

....

....

....

....

15 its quite cute said pippa

....

....

....

Answers and explanations on page 117

An odd-looking creature

The platypus is an odd-looking creature. It's a furry mammal but it has a bill like a duck and webbed feet. It doesn't have teeth. The platypus paddles with its front feet and steers with its back feet and tail. Its nostrils close underwater. The platypus uses its bill to sense where it is going. Males have venomous heel spurs on their back feet.

A platypus eats insects, worms, shellfish and larvae. It uses its bill to scoop food, along with mud and small rocks, from the bottom of ponds. Because it doesn't have teeth, the platypus uses the rocks to grind the food in its bill into smaller bits.

A female lays one or two eggs in a burrow. She keeps her eggs warm by holding them between her body and her tail. Babies can swim on their own when they are about three or four months old.

The platypus only lives along the east coast of Australia. Its future is uncertain because the places where it lives are being destroyed to build houses for people. Some platypuses also get caught and drown in yabby traps that people leave in creeks and rivers.

A platypus with a worm

1 The text is
- A a story.
- B a news report.
- C an information report.

2 The writer of the text
- A is not well informed about the platypus.
- B is well informed about the platypus.
- C uses technical terms that do not suit the text.

3 Connect the paragraphs to suitable subheadings.

Paragraph 1	A Its conservation status
Paragraph 2	B How it breeds
Paragraph 3	C What it looks like
Paragraph 4	D How it eats

4 Complete the similes. The platypus
- A has a bill like a ……………………… .
- B has webbed feet like a ……………………… .
- C has fur like a ……………………… .
- D lays eggs like a ……………………… .
- E has a burrow like a ……………………… .

5 Why might a male platypus have venomous heal spurs? Choose **all** that apply.
- A to fight off other males
- B to fight off females
- C to kill its prey

6 How can we make sure that platypuses don't become extinct?

………………………………………………

………………………………………………

Get creative

7 Write a report about an animal. Write paragraphs that tell what it is, where it lives, what it eats and its status.

Answers and explanations on page 117

Bush medicine

For thousands of years, First Nations Australians have used native plants as medicine.

Here are some bush remedies:

Tea-tree leaves can be crushed to make a paste that heals cuts and sores. (Tea-tree oil is a strong antiseptic that kills germs.)

Emu-bush leaves can be used on cuts and sores.

Gumbi Gumbi leaf tea can help fight coughs and colds.

Umbrella bush wattle bark can be soaked and boiled and the liquid used as a cough medicine.

Kangaroo apples, eaten raw or cooked, can help with joint pain.

Australian native lemongrass leaves, stems and roots can be used in a tea to help with sore throats and headaches.

Eucalyptus can be used for pain relief.

Scientists have only recently realised just how good some of these traditional medicines are. They are excited to discover more about these age-old remedies.

Tea-tree leaves

1 Which plant provides a strong antiseptic? ....

2 Which **two** plants can be used to make cough medicine? ....

....

3 Which items can bush medicine be made from? Choose **all** that apply.

A fruit
B insects
C leaves
D stems
E roots
F bark

4 Medicines from which of the following plants are applied to skin?

A tea-tree
B umbrella bush wattle
C Gumbi Gumbi
D emu bush
E kangaroo apple
F native lemongrass
G eucalyptus

5 Medicines from which of the following plants are swallowed?

A tea-tree
B umbrella bush wattle
C Gumbi Gumbi
D emu bush
E kangaroo apple
F native lemongrass
G eucalyptus

6 Would you be happy to try a bush medicine? Explain.

....

....

Answers and explanations on page 118

SPELLING

Write the correct spelling of the underlined words in questions 1–4.

1 Bush medisin can be very useful.

....

2 Tea-tree oil is an antaseptic.

....

3 Make lemongrass tea for a sore throwt.

....

4 Use kangaroo apples for releef from joint pain.

....

5 Write three words from the word family that includes **strong**.

....

....

VOCABULARY

6 Circle the answer that has the nearest meaning to the underlined words.

Gumbi Gumbi leaf tea helps fight coughs and colds.

A combat B heal
C cure D create

7 Write a word from the text to match the meaning.

something that kills germs

....

8 Add a word from the text to complete the sentence.

Scientists are excited about traditional

....

9 Circle the word that does **not** belong.

A cough B cold
C flu D sore

GRAMMAR

10 Complete the sentence with a noun group.

....
can be used in a tea.

11 Write past tense verbs to complete the sentence.

We .... and
.... the wattle bark.

12 Complete the sentence with a prepositional phrase that tells **where**, **when** or **how**.

....

....

First Nations Australians have used bush medicine.

13 Add a conjunction to correctly join the clauses.

Drink Gumbi Gumbi tea ....
do not drink tea-tree oil.

PUNCTUATION

Rewrite the sentences correctly.

14 leaves stems and roots are used to make tea

....

....

....

15 first nations australians use bush medicine said ethan

....

....

....

Answers and explanations on page 118

Bush medicine

For thousands of years, First Nations Australians have used native plants as medicine.

Here are some bush remedies:

Tea-tree leaves can be crushed to make a paste that heals cuts and sores. (Tea-tree oil is a strong antiseptic that kills germs.)

Emu-bush leaves can be used on cuts and sores.

Gumbi Gumbi leaf tea can help fight coughs and colds.

Umbrella bush wattle bark can be soaked and boiled and the liquid used as a cough medicine.

Kangaroo apples, eaten raw or cooked, can help with joint pain.

Australian native lemongrass leaves, stems and roots can be used in a tea to help with sore throats and headaches.

Eucalyptus can be used for pain relief.

Scientists have only recently realised just how good some of these traditional medicines are. They are excited to discover more about these age-old remedies.

Tea-tree leaves

1 The text is
- A a story.
- B a news report.
- C an information report.

2 The writer of the text is
- A a First Nations person.
- B a scientist.
- C a person interested in bush medicine.

3 The text has
- A an introduction and persuasive arguments to make you use bush medicine.
- B an introduction, information and a concluding statement.
- C an orientation, a list of plants and a call to action to try the medicines.

4 In line 15, 'They' refers to
- A traditional medicines.
- B First Nations Australians.
- C scientists.

5 What information would you need if you wanted to make one of the remedies? Choose **all** that apply.
- A where to find the plants
- B quantities of the plant needed
- C warnings about the plants or medicine
- D how to use the medicine
- E how much the medicine costs
- F a recipe for making the medicine

6 Why are scientists excited about bush medicine?

....

....

7 Research one bush medicine. Write a report.

Answers and explanations on page 118

READING AND COMPREHENSION

The Spider and the Fly

by Mary Howitt (published 1829)

'Will you walk into my parlour?'
Said a spider to a fly;
''Tis the prettiest little parlour
That ever you did spy.
The way into my parlour
Is up a winding stair,
And I have many pretty things
To show you when you're there.'
'O no, no,' said the little fly,
'To ask me is in vain;
For who goes up your winding stair
Can ne'er come down again.'

'I'm sure you must be weary
With soaring up so high;
Will you rest upon my little bed?'
Said the spider to the fly.
'There are pretty curtains drawn around;
The sheets are fine and thin;
And if you like to rest awhile,
I'll snugly tuck you in.'
'O no, no,' said the little fly,
'For I've often heard it said
They never, never wake again,
Who sleep upon your bed.'

1 When was the poem published?

....

2 Choose **all** that apply. The spider offers
- **A** to show pretty things in the parlour.
- **B** a rest upon a little bed.
- **C** something to eat.

3 Choose **all** that apply. The spider is
- **A** charming.
- **B** cunning.
- **C** deceitful.
- **D** determined.

4 Choose **all** that apply. The fly is
- **A** smart.
- **B** silly.
- **C** easily persuaded.
- **D** strong-willed.

5 Choose **all** that apply. The spider's voice would sound
- **A** smooth.
- **B** harsh.
- **C** kindly.
- **D** angry.
- **E** loud.
- **F** sweet.

6 Is the spider kind? Explain.

....

....

....

....

....

....

Answers and explanations on page 118

SPELLING

Write the correct spelling of the underlined words in questions 1–4.

1 'Tis the prittiest little parlour

....

2 With sawing up so high

....

3 My parlour is up a whinding stair

....

4 I've often herd it said

....

5 Write three words from the word family that includes **sleeps**.

....

....

....

VOCABULARY

6 Circle the answer that has the nearest meaning to the underlined word.

'O no, no,' said the little fly.

A asked B commanded
C questioned D announced

7 Write a word from the text to match the meaning.

of the highest quality

....

8 Add a word from the text to complete the sentence.

There are pretty curtains .... around.

9 Circle the word that does **not** belong.

A snugly B cosily
C tightly D warmly

GRAMMAR

10 Complete the sentence with a noun group.

'Will you rest upon ....?' said the spider to the fly.

11 Write a past tense verb to complete the sentence.

The spider .... a mosquito in its web.

12 Complete the sentence with a prepositional phrase.

The way into the parlour is ....

....

13 Add a conjunction to correctly join the clauses.

'I'll tuck you in .... I'll draw the curtains,' promised the spider.

PUNCTUATION

Rewrite the sentences correctly.

14 will you come into my parlour asked a spider

....

....

....

15 I have a cosy bed for a fly declared the spider

....

....

....

Answers and explanations on page 118

TEXTS IN CONTEXT

The Spider and the Fly

by Mary Howitt (published 1829)

'Will you walk into my parlour?'
Said a spider to a fly;
''Tis the prettiest little parlour
That ever you did spy.
The way into my parlour
Is up a winding stair,
And I have many pretty things
To show you when you're there.'
'O no, no,' said the little fly,
'To ask me is in vain;
For who goes up your winding stair
Can ne'er come down again.'

'I'm sure you must be weary
With soaring up so high;
Will you rest upon my little bed?'
Said the spider to the fly.
'There are pretty curtains drawn around;
The sheets are fine and thin;
And if you like to rest awhile,
I'll snugly tuck you in.'
'O no, no,' said the little fly,
'For I've often heard it said
They never, never wake again,
Who sleep upon your bed.'

1 The text is
A entertaining.
B educational.
C informative.

2 The audience for the text is likely
A scientists.
B children.
C adults.

3 Why is there an illustration and not a photo?

....

....

....

4 The poem is written as a conversation between
A a spider and a fly.
B a spider, a fly and the poet.
C a spider, a fly and a narrator.

5 'To ask me is in vain' (line 12)
What does this mean?
A It's pointless to ask.
B It's thoughtful to ask.
C It's vain of you to ask.

6 What does the spider want?
A to be friends with the fly
B to eat the fly
C to show the fly the pretty things in the parlour

7 Write a poem that is a conversation between animals.

Answers and explanations on page 118

News in review

TV host: We are here today to talk about shark nets at our beaches. My guest is shark expert, Professor Sofia Hamden. What do you think about shark nets, Professor Hamden?

Professor Hamden: I do not agree with shark nets. Very few people get killed by sharks. People fear sharks unnecessarily. Most sharks are harmless to people but they get caught in nets and die. More importantly, shark nets trap and kill whales, turtles and dolphins. These animals drown when they get caught in the nets.

TV host: People think the nets keep the beaches safe.

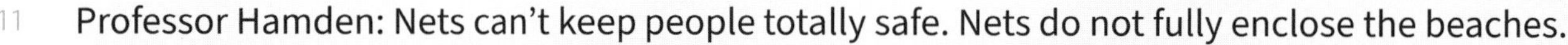

Professor Hamden: Nets can't keep people totally safe. Nets do not fully enclose the beaches. Sharks can swim around them. It's best to use modern technology to keep people safe. For example, electronic devices can repel sharks. Drones and gyrocopters can be used to monitor beaches and sound alerts if a shark is nearby.

Many shark species are endangered because humans kill too many sharks for food. Oceans need sharks. Every species in the food chain is needed to keep the ocean healthy. We should not use shark nets.

1 Name **three** ways of using modern technology to help keep people safe from sharks.

....

....

2 A healthy food chain needs ....

3 Why is Professor Hamden being interviewed?

....

4 How do electronic devices work?

A They catch sharks. B They kill sharks. C They repel sharks.

5 What is Professor Hamden's main concern?

A Nets kill sharks.
B Nets kill whales, turtles and dolphins.
C Nets don't protect swimmers.

6 To get a balance of views, who else should be interviewed about shark nets?

....

....

Answers and explanations on page 118

SPELLING

Write the correct spelling of the underlined words in questions 1–4.

1 People fear sharks unecesarily.

....

2 Sharks are essenshal for healthy oceans.

....

3 Shark species are endangerd.

....

4 We can now use modern teknology.

....

5 Write three words from the word family that includes **enclose**.

....

....

....

VOCABULARY

6 Circle the answer that has the nearest meaning to the underlined words.

Drones can monitor beaches.

A supervise B watch
C instruct D guide

7 Write a word from the text to match the meaning.

drive away or repulse

....

8 Add a word from the text to complete the sentence.

People fear sharks ....

9 Circle the word or word group that does **not** belong.

A open up B surround
C encompass D enclose

GRAMMAR

10 Complete the sentence with a noun group.

....

get killed by sharks.

11 Write a verb group to complete the sentence.

Gyrocopters ....

to monitor beaches.

12 Complete the sentence with a prepositional phrase that tells **where**.

Animals drown when they are caught

....

13 Add a conjunction to correctly join the clauses.

Shark nets are being used to protect beaches

....

they don't fully enclose them.

PUNCTUATION

Rewrite the sentences correctly.

14 many harmless animals get tangled and die said sofia

....

....

....

15 what do you think about netting asked philip

....

....

....

Answers and explanations on pages 118–119

News in review

TV host: We are here today to talk about shark nets at our beaches. My guest is shark expert, Professor Sofia Hamden. What do you think about shark nets, Professor Hamden?

Professor Hamden: I do not agree with shark nets. Very few people get killed by sharks. People fear sharks unnecessarily. Most sharks are harmless to people but they get caught in nets and die. More importantly, shark nets trap and kill whales, turtles and dolphins. These animals drown when they get caught in the nets.

TV host: People think the nets keep the beaches safe.

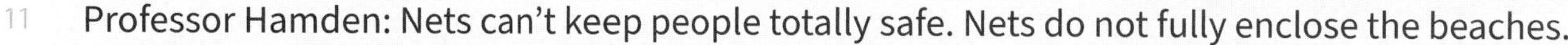

Professor Hamden: Nets can't keep people totally safe. Nets do not fully enclose the beaches. Sharks can swim around them. It's best to use modern technology to keep people safe. For example, electronic devices can repel sharks. Drones and gyrocopters can be used to monitor beaches and sound alerts if a shark is nearby.

Many shark species are endangered because humans kill too many sharks for food. Oceans need sharks. Every species in the food chain is needed to keep the ocean healthy. We should not use shark nets.

1 Professor Hamden's purpose is to
- A persuade people not to use nets.
- B explain how nets kill animals.
- C inform people about sharks.

2 The audience for the text is
- A children in classrooms.
- B people who watch television news.
- C shark experts.

3 The text is an interview. Its structure is
- A an introduction and then a speech.
- B an introduction then question and answer.
- C a news report which includes an opinion.

4 Which animals does the pronoun **these** refer to in lines 7–9 below?

More importantly, shark nets trap and kill whales, turtles and dolphins. These animals drown when they get caught in the nets.

....

....

5 Why would the Professor believe that people fear sharks unnecessarily?

....

....

....

6 If the decision to use shark nets was yours to make, what would you do? Explain.

....

....

....

7 Write a news report about people rescuing a baby whale caught in a shark net.

Answers and explanations on page 119

The Shy albatross

Shy albatrosses are sea birds. They range across the southern oceans then come back to three islands off the coast of Tasmania every year to breed.

In the past, albatrosses were killed for their feathers to make hats. In 1909 there were only 300 pairs left on Albatross Island. Now there are about 5000 pairs but they face further threats. They starve when their stomachs fill up with plastic. They drown when they get caught in fishing lines. And, because of climate change, shy albatrosses now have difficulty finding materials for their nests and food. Sometimes they have to lay their eggs on the ground. Then the eggs and chicks have no protection from harsh weather. Many of the chicks die.

Scientists, conservationists and park rangers decided they had to help the abatrosses cope with the impact of climate change. They had concrete nests made and they placed the nests along the cliff tops of Albatross Island. They hoped the birds would use the artificial nests and they have. The birds have even added mud and vegetation to the nests to improve them. Albatross eggs and chicks now have a better chance of surviving.

1. Albatrosses were once killed to make
   - **A** feathers.
   - **B** hats.
   - **C** fish bait.

2. Where do shy albatrosses breed? ....

3. Choose **all** that apply. Albatrosses use the concrete nests because they
   - **A** recognise a sturdy nest when they see one.
   - **B** are too lazy to make their own.
   - **C** realise that concrete nests are better than the hard, bare ground.

4. How do albatrosses die when they get caught in fishing lines?

   ....

5. Choose **all** that apply. How is climate change affecting albatrosses?
   - **A** They are making artificial nests.
   - **B** Their eggs aren't hatching due to the weather.
   - **C** Their chicks are dying of cold.
   - **D** They can't find enough food.
   - **E** They can't find enough materials to make good nests.

6. Who is to blame for the albatross's problems?

   ....

Answers and explanations on page 119

SPELLING

Write the correct spelling of the underlined words in questions 1–4.

1 Consavationists are helping albatrosses.

2 They need help serviving climate change.

3 Nests are made using vegatation.

4 Climate change makes it diffacult for the birds.

5 Write three words from the word family that includes **return**.

VOCABULARY

6 Circle the answer that has the nearest meaning to the underlined words.

There aren't enough nesting materials.

A grass
B fabric
C eggs
D items

7 Write a word from the text to match the meaning.

a young bird

8 Add a word from the text to complete the sentence.

Without a good nest, chicks have no ______ from bad weather.

9 Circle the word that does **not** belong.

A artificial
B real
C manufactured
D fake

GRAMMAR

10 Complete the sentence with a noun group.

______ had artificial nests made.

11 Write a past tense verb to complete the sentence.

The birds ______ mud and vegetation to the nests.

12 Complete the sentence with a prepositional phrase that tells **when**.

They return to their same nests ______.

13 Add a conjunction to correctly join the clauses.

______ of climate change, the shy albatross is in trouble.

PUNCTUATION

Rewrite the sentences correctly.

14 they breed on albatross island said lexi

15 do they like their new nests asked louis

Answers and explanations on page 119

The Shy albatross

Shy albatrosses are sea birds. They range across the southern oceans then come back to three islands off the coast of Tasmania every year to breed.

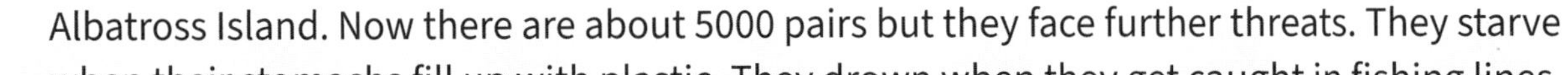

In the past, albatrosses were killed for their feathers to make hats. In 1909 there were only 300 pairs left on Albatross Island. Now there are about 5000 pairs but they face further threats. They starve when their stomachs fill up with plastic. They drown when they get caught in fishing lines. And, because of climate change, shy albatrosses now have difficulty finding materials for their nests and food. Sometimes they have to lay their eggs on the ground. Then the eggs and chicks have no protection from harsh weather. Many of the chicks die.

Scientists, conservationists and park rangers decided they had to help the abatrosses cope with the impact of climate change. They had concrete nests made and they placed the nests along the cliff tops of Albatross Island. They hoped the birds would use the artificial nests and they have. The birds have even added mud and vegetation to the nests to improve them. Albatross eggs and chicks now have a better chance of surviving.

1 The text
- A entertains.
- B informs.
- C instructs.
- D persuades.

2 Who might find this text interesting?
- A anyone interested in birds
- B anyone interested in travelling to Tasmania's islands
- C anyone interested in storms and climate change

3 Link each paragraph number to a statement.

Paragraph 1	A Some people are trying to help albatrosses.
Paragraph 2	B People cause problems for albatrosses.
Paragraph 3	C The shy albatross flies a long way.

4 'They hoped the birds would use the artificial nests' (line 14).

Who does the pronoun **they** refer to in the text? Choose **all** that apply.
- A scientists
- B park rangers
- C shy albatrosses
- D conservationists
- E the writer of the text

5 The albatrosses return each year to the three islands to breed. Where are they the rest of the year?

....

6 What do you think about people killing birds to use their feathers for hats?

....

....

....

....

Get creative

7 Find out about another animal that is killed for fashion. Write a report.

Answers and explanations on page 119

The stolen generations

From early in the 1800s to around 1970 many Aboriginal and Torres Strait Islander children were taken from their families. The government ordered the children to be taken from their families. They were taken against their wishes and against the wishes of their parents. These children are called the stolen generations. Many government officials had no respect for, or understanding of, Aboriginal culture or people.

The children were put in orphanages or given to non-Aboriginal foster parents. Most of them never saw their families again. Brothers and sisters were often separated too. The children had to speak English. They were usually punished if they spoke their native languages. They were unable to learn traditional knowledge from their parents or grandparents, so this knowledge was lost to generations of Aboriginal people.

Older children were put to work as domestic servants or farmhands. They were made to work for free.

The trauma suffered by the stolen generations is still felt today by many Aboriginal and Torres Strait Islander people.

1 Choose **all** that apply. Older children worked as

A servants.
B farmhands.
C teachers.

2 Choose **all** that apply. Who did most of the stolen generations never see again?

A their siblings
B their parents
C their families
D their children

3 Choose **all** that apply. A domestic servant would likely have to

A wash dishes.
B sweep floors.
C make beds.

4 Why do you think the stolen generations weren't allowed to speak their native languages?

....

....

5 How do some Aboriginal people feel today about the stolen generations?

Choose **all** that might apply.

A angry
B sad
C frightened

6 Choose **all** that apply. Removing the children from their home environment was

A sensible.
B terrible.
C cruel.

7 Choose **all** that apply. Imagine being taken from your family. How do you think you would feel?

A frightened
B worried
C angry
D happy
E sad
F calm
G trusting
H joyous
I excited

Answers and explanations on page 119

Each sentence has one word that is incorrect. Write the correct spelling of the underlined word in the box.

1 Aboriginil children were stolen.

2 They were stolen from their familys.

3 They were unable to learn their tradishinal languages.

4 They are called the stolen genarations.

5 The children suffared.

Read the text below. Choose the correct verb or verb group to complete the sentences.

The children (6) stolen from their people. The trauma (7) still affecting Aboriginal and Torres Strait Islander people today. The government of 2008 said sorry that the children (8) all those years ago.

6 A was B is C were D are

7 A was B are C is D has

8 A are stolen B will have stolen C is stolen D were stolen

9 Choose the correct article to complete the sentence.

They were stolen against .... wishes of their parents.

A a B an C the

10 Which verb group correctly completes the sentence?

The stolen generations .... if they spoke their native languages.

A usually punish
B is usually punished
C were usually punished
D are used to being punished

11 Which word connects the clauses?

The government took the children .... it had no respect for Aboriginal culture.

A although
B until
C so
D because

12 Which pronoun correctly completes the sentence?

Older children worked as domestic servants or farmhands. .... were not paid.

A Them
B They
C She
D We

13 Which sentence is punctuated correctly?

A Aboriginal and Torres Strait islander children were taken from their families.
B They are the stolen Generations.
C The Government thought it was a good idea at the time.
D Brothers and sisters were usually separated.

14 Which sentence is punctuated correctly?

A 'Its very sad,' said Matilda.
B 'It would have been terrible for children and parents,' said Alfie.
C 'Why would they do it? asked Rose.'
D 'I can't imagine it,' said Frank?

Answers and explanations on page 119

ANSWERS

Unit 1A PAGE 8

1. **C**. See line 2.
2. **B**. Se lines 2 and 6.
3. **B**. You can work out that the bakery is a shop.
4. **A**, **B**, **E** and **F**. You can work out that four ingredients are used in the jam. **C** and **D** are incorrect because a saucepan and stove are tools not ingredients.
5. **A**. You can work out that the jam is kept in jars because Josh poured the cooled jam 'into really clean jars', i.e. for storing.
6. You can judge that Mum was very happy because Josh writes 'Mum loved my jam'.

Unit 1B PAGE 9

1. birthday
2. sugar
3. Pour
4. saucepan
5. mix, mixing, mixture
6. **C**.
7. dissolved
8. clean
9. **B**.
10. scones
11. **C**.
12. into really clean jars/into jars
13. **D**.
14. I made jam for Mum.
15. Who likes scones?

Unit 1C PAGE 10

1. **B**.
2. **C**.
3. **C**.
4. Teacher/parent to check
5. **B**. The text is about Josh making jam as a birthday treat for Mum.
6. **A** and **B**. You can judge that **A** and **B** are the reasons Josh decided to cook jam. **C** is likely true but not the reason he decided to cook jam.
7. Responses will vary. Suggested answers: Wash your hands to get rid of germs. Be careful with the hot stove. Don't leave anything to burn on the stove. Don't put anything near the stove that might catch fire, e.g. tea towels. Use an oven mitt when handling hot items. Be careful with knives. Pick up knives by the handle not the sharp end. Wipe up floor spills so you don't slip over. Don't put water on a cooking-oil fire—it makes the fire worse. If a fire starts, call 000.

Unit 2A PAGE 11

1. **C** and **E**. See line 6.
2. **B**. See line 15.
3. **B**. You can work out that Mia would prefer the top bunk because she sleeps there whenever her sister is away from home.
4. **C**. You can work out that Mia is likely to be a good swimmer because she lists swimming as one of her favourite hobbies/interests, and because she likes the idea of being a dolphin and swimming all day.
5. **A**. You can work out that Mia thinks dolphins have a good life because she'd like to be one so she can swim and play all day with friends and family.
6. Responses will vary. You can judge that Mia values family and kindness to animals the most. She seems to have loving relationships with Mum and Harper. She mentions love between dolphins as a good reason to be a dolphin. She wants to help animals when she grows up.

Unit 2B PAGE 12

1. colour
2. swimming
3. friend
4. bedroom
5. Suggested answers: sleeps, sleeping, slept, sleeper, sleepy, sleepily
6. **A**.
7. hobby
8. subject
9. **D**.
10. dolphin
11. **D**.
12. on Harper's bunk/in Harper's bed/on the top bunk
13. **C**.
14. Sometimes Harper has a sleepover.
15. Mia lives in Drummoyne.

Unit 2C PAGE 13

1. **B**.
2. **C** and **D**.
3. **D**.
4. **A**.
5. Responses will vary. You might like Mia as a friend because you like animals too. Or you might decide she is not the type of person you would choose as a friend because you do not have the same interests.

6. Responses will vary. You might dislike Mia sleeping in your bed because your bed is your own and you like it all to yourself. Or you might be happy to share with Mia because you have the bed every other night and you don't need it if you are on a sleepover.
7. Responses will vary.

Unit 3A PAGE 14

1. **B**. See line 2.
2. **C**. See line 3.
3. **C**. You can work out that it's Scoobie who's locked up.
4. **A** and **C**. You can work out that the dog misses Jackie while she is at work. Dad tells Liam that Scoobie is bored and lonely. **B** is incorrect. There is no evidence to suggest that Mr Timble yells at Scoobie.
5. **A.** You can work out that Liam thinks going to the park will make Scoobie happy.
6. You can judge that Dad is most concerned about Scoobie. He wants to make sure Scoobie is safe and happy. He says it isn't fair for Scoobie to be locked up in a unit all day.

Unit 3B PAGE 15

1. upstairs
2. across
3. fair
4. afternoon
5. Suggested answers: bore, bores, boring, boredom
6. **C**.
7. responsibility
8. Council
9. **A**.
10. neighbour
11. **D**.
12. in the unit/up in the unit
13. **A**.
14. Be quiet!
15. Can we help?

Unit 3C PAGE 16

1. **B**.
2. **A**.
3. **A**, **C** and **D**.
4. Problem: Scoobie is lonely and bored so he barks all day. This upsets Mr Timble.
   Possible solution: Take Scoobie to the park every day so he is not so bored or lonely.
   Extra solution: Responses will vary. Suggested answers: Ask Mr Timble to mind Scoobie. He might be bored and lonely too. Tell Jackie so that she can do something else with Scoobie while she is at work. Dad might take Scoobie into his and Liam's unit each day.
5. **B**.
6. Responses will vary. Suggested answers: Mr Timble should report Scoobie to the Council because Scoobie is unhappy and the council will make Jackie sort something out. Mr Timble should not report Scoobie to the Council because Jackie has to go to work and has nowhere else to leave Scoobie.
7. Responses will vary.

Unit 4A PAGE 17

1. 1896 (See line 2.)
2. Hilaire Belloc (See line 2.)
3. **B**.
4. **C** and **D**.
5. **B**. You can work out that there are no dodos left in the world because they are extinct.
6. Responses will vary. You might judge that the illustrations are funny or clever and suit the poems. You might comment that the museum drawing only shows adult men visiting the museum in 1896.

Unit 4B PAGE 18

1. beast
2. large
3. squawk
4. dumb
5. Suggested answers: marvelled, marvelling, marvellous, marvellously, marvellousness
6. **C**.
7. museum
8. trunk
9. **C**.
10. beast
11. **D**.
12. in the museum/in a museum
13. **B**.
14. Why did it disappear?
15. Look there!

Unit 4C PAGE 19

1. **C**.
2. **B**.
3. changing font and letter size: little LARGE
   alliteration: beast before behind; squawk squeak; bones beak
4. mind—behind; more—before; around—ground; air—there; squeak—beak; dumb—Mu-se-um.
5. **A**.
6. **B**.
7. Responses will vary.

ANSWERS

Unit 5A PAGE 20

1. 4–6 pm Saturday 10 April (See line 6.)
2. unexpected/out of the blue (See lines 9 and 15–16.)
3. **C**. You can work out that money raised will be donated to the charity UNICEF to help children in need.
4. **C**. You can work out that Lexi is the main singer because she describes herself as in the middle in the photo. This is confirmed by the fact that the girl third from the left in the photo does not have an instrument and is holding a microphone.
5. **B**. You can work out that Mum was surprised because she 'said that it was unexpected'.
6. You can judge from the photo and the information on the poster that the band members are likely to be confident because they are going to perform in front of an audience. They are well organised because they formed a band, made posters to promote the concert and likely organise themselves to practise their music regularly.

Unit 5B PAGE 21

1. Entry
2. money
3. portable
4. music
5. Suggested answers: expect, expected, expectant, expecting, unexpectedly
6. **C**.
7. UNICEF
8. portable
9. **B**.
10. concert
11. **B**.
12. in France
13. **D**.
14. The concert is at 10 Beatie St.
15. Are you going on Saturday?

Unit 5C PAGE 22

1. **A**.
2. **A**, **B** and **C**.
3. **B** and **C**. What is on, the date and time, and the address must be included on a poster to advertise an event. **D** could also be correct: why the event is being held, such as to raise money for charity, would be important. **F** could also be correct: who to contact about the event might also be useful.
4. BEST, great
5. **C**.
6. Responses will vary.
7. Responses will vary. Posters need to include information about what's on, where (address) and when (date and time). You might also include a reason to explain why the concert is being held if you think this is relevant to your audience.

Unit 6A PAGE 23

1. **A**, **C**, **F** and **G**. See lines 3–6. (**B** is incorrect as Alex does not have a temperature. **D** and **E** are incorrect because Alex only says he might have these.)
2. **B**. See line 7.
3. **C**. You can work out that Mum wants to help Alex overcome his nervous feelings by breathing deeply to calm down. Being nervous or stressed can make your heart beat faster.
4. **A**. You can work out that Alex does really feel sick even though he is likely not sick, just worried or nervous or stressed.
5. **A**. You can work out that Mum remains calm and speaks calmly to Alex.
6. You can imagine that Alex might be worried about school for reasons such as being bullied, having a new teacher, having no friends, being in a new class or having trouble with schoolwork.

Unit 6B PAGE 24

1. temperature
2. might
3. breath
4. something
5. Suggested answers: sicken, sickened, sickening, sickly
6. **C**.
7. clammy
8. diarrhoea
9. **D**.
10. heart
11. **C**.
12. at school
13. **B**.
14. Now breathe out: 1, 2, 3, 4, 5.
15. Mum thinks Alex has a problem at school.

Unit 6C PAGE 25

1. **C**.
2. **B**.
3. like a balloon
4. diarrhoea, temperature, clammy, vomit
5. **B**.
6. Responses will vary.
7. Responses will vary.

Unit 7A PAGE 26

1. **B**. See line 3.
2. **B** and **C**. See lines 2 and 4.
3. **A**. You can work out that the dog seems clever because of the things it does when the children communicate with it.

4. **A**. You can work out that the children are most impressed with the dog's attitude towards the remote control.
5. **B**. You can work out that the dog seems to understand English. It cannot speak English and there's nothing in the text to suggest it wants to learn English.
6. It barks yes and no. It sits in Dad's seat. It seems to know colours. It keeps the remote control.

Unit 7B — PAGE 27

1. fluttered
2. shelves
3. some
4. homework
5. Suggested answers: question, questioned, questioning, questioningly, questionable
6. **D**.
7. scanned
8. remote control
9. **C**.
10. (floating) chairs
11. **C**.
12. from Dad's bedroom
13. **B**.
14. Is that Dad?
15. The dog sat in their father's seat.

Unit 7C — PAGE 28

1. **B**.
2. **C**.
3. **B**.
4. **A**. (**C** could also be correct because the children seem very relaxed and unconcerned in the photo.)
5. **C**.
6. **B**. The books are described as floating and fluttering. These movements are gentle. The children look relaxed and not upset or panicking. The setting in the photo is well lit and not scary.
7. Responses will vary.

NAPLAN-style Reading Test 1 — PAGE 29

1. **B**. See line 2.
2. **D**. See lines 15–16.
3. **C**.
4. **C**.
5. **A**, **B** and **D**.
6. **D**. You can judge that Rose thinks if she says she was joking then she can get away with being mean. It's an excuse so people think she did not really mean what she said. Being mean to, or about, other children is not a joke.
7. **A**, **B**, **C** and **E**.

NAPLAN-style Conventions of Language Test 1 — PAGE 30

1. whispering
2. joking
3. friends
4. laugh
5. jealous
6. **A**.
7. **C**.
8. **B**.
9. **B**.
10. **C**.
11. **C**.
12. **B**.
13. **D**.
14. **C**

Unit 8A — PAGE 31

1. **C**. See lines 6–8.
2. **A**. See lines 8–9.
3. **C**. You can work out that all the rocky areas are covered by water at high tide but when the tide goes out, it leaves pools of water behind. Living creatures survive there until the tide comes back in.
4. **C**.
5. **A**, **B** and **C**.
6. You can judge that the writer wants people to respect the creatures that live in rock pools by looking and not touching, and by not disturbing their environment.

Unit 8B — PAGE 32

1. octopus
2. touch
3. creature
4. environment
5. Suggested answers: danger, dangerously, endangered, endangering
6. **B**.
7. poisonous
8. pools
9. **D**.
10. dangerous
11. **B**.
12. in rock pools/in a rock pool
13. **C**.
14. Why can't we touch things in a rock pool?
15. It's better to leave things alone.

Unit 8C — PAGE 33

1. **B**.
2. **C**.
3. **C**.
4. rock pool, tide, crabs, sea stars, limpets, sea snails, blue-ringed octopus, poisonous, environment, tidal salt water

5. suffer, kind, harm, survive
6. Responses will vary but you should recognise that one child is breaking the first rule: 'Look but don't touch.' Apart from disturbing the creatures she is at risk of touching a blue-ringed octopus.
7. Responses will vary.

Unit 9A PAGE 34

1. **C**. See line 2.
2. **C**. See line 5.
3. **A**. You can work out that the tentacles sting.
4. **C**. You can work out that the tentacles keep stinging.
5. **B**. You can infer that rips are the most common risk at a beach.
6. You can judge that the differently coloured flags are all there to keep people safe. The red and yellow flags tell people where to swim and the red-and-white flags tell people when they have to stay out of the water.

Unit 9B PAGE 35

1. Lifeguards
2. closed
3. Huge
4. swimmers
5. Suggested answers: carry, carried, carrying, carrier
6. **A**.
7. prey
8. tentacles
9. **D**.
10. dangerous
11. **B**.
12. between the red and yellow flags
13. **D**.
14. What is best for a bluebottle sting?
15. Lifeguards helped Matilda.

Unit 9C PAGE 36

1. **B**.
2. **B**.
3. **C**.
4. 1 **B**. 2 **D**. 3 **C**. 4 **A**.
5. **A**.
6. **A** and **C**.
7. Responses will vary.

Unit 10A PAGE 37

1. **B**. See line 2.
2. **C**. See line 4.
3. **B**. You can work out that extinct animals were sculpted because the theme of the event was extinction.
4. **C**. You can work out that the biodegradable glue helps hold the sculptures together temporarily ('for a while anyway').
5. **B**. You can work out that carving sculptures from sand is only possible because the sand is compacted.
6. You can judge that she liked the sculptures she saw. She thinks she'd enjoy it and she thinks she'd be good at it.

Unit 10B PAGE 38

1. sculptures
2. extinction
3. worked
4. voted
5. Suggested answers: deliver, delivering, delivery, deliverance
6. **D**.
7. artist
8. rhinoceros/West African Black rhinoceros
9. **C**.
10. professional
11. **C**.
12. from a quarry
13. **B**.
14. Gillen liked the West African Black rhino sculpture best.
15. The dinosaur sculpture wasn't her favourite.

Unit 10C PAGE 39

1. **B**.
2. **A**, **C** and **D**.
3. **B**.
4. **B**. You can work out that Gillen means moon because she added a moon drawing next to her name.
5. **B**.
6. **C**.
7. Responses will vary.

Unit 11A PAGE 40

1. **C**. See line 15.
2. **A**. See lines 2–3 and 7.
3. **B**. You can work out that Hugo had never met his Uncle because the text says it had been 20 years since Hugo's mum had seen Norman. **A** is incorrect: Mum is only going to be working overseas for three months. **C** is incorrect because Mum really does need someone to look after Hugo while she is overseas.
4. **B**. You can work out that Mum knows her brother is a sweetie.
5. **C**. You can work out that Mum is having doubts about leaving Norman at the house.
6. You can judge that Mum is a bit concerned because Hugo says she didn't look very confident and she hesitates, not moving towards the house.

ANSWERS

Unit 11B PAGE 41

1. doesn't
2. believe
3. address
4. worried
5. Suggested answers: belief, disbelief, believes, believing, believed, believable, unbelievable
6. C.
7. haunted
8. uncle
9. B.
10. black
11. C.
12. beside his mother/in front of the house
13. C.
14. It wasn't a joke.
15. 'It looks scary,' said Mum.

Unit 11C PAGE 42

1. **B.**
2. C.
3. **B.**
4. **B.**
5. **A**, **B**, C, **D** and **F.**
6. Responses will vary. You might say no because you don't know your uncle at all and the house looks spooky. You might say yes because it seems like it could be an adventure and it might be fun.
7. Responses will vary.

Unit 12A PAGE 43

1. skin cancer/melanoma (See lines 8–10.)
2. melanoma (See lines 3–5.)
3. Responses will vary. Suggested answers: indoors, under a tree, under a roof or awning, under an umbrella
4. **A.**
5. C.
6. You can judge that Abigail thinks he's lucky because the melanoma was small so it was possible to cut it out before the cancer spread.

Unit 12B PAGE 44

1. cancer
2. Protect
3. Australians
4. hadn't
5. Suggested answers: damage, damaged, damages
6. C.
7. protect
8. body
9. C.
10. strongest
11. **D.**
12. anywhere/through his body/ anywhere in his body
13. **B.**
14. That's when the sun is strongest.
15. The sun can be deadly in Australia.

Unit 12C PAGE 45

1. C.
2. C.
3. Slip, Slop, Slap, Seek, Stay, Slide; skin, SPF30+, sunscreen, shade, sun, strongest, skin, sunglasses
4. C.
5. Because skin cancer could have killed Abigail's father, she has learned a lot about the subject and wants other people to understand the importance of sun protection.
6. **B.**
7. Responses will vary.

Unit 13A PAGE 46

1. air, water (See lines 3–4.)
2. termites, ticks, flies, cockroaches (See lines 6–7.)
3. C.
4. **B.** You can work out that loss of habitat can cause a species to become extinct.
5. **A.** You can work out that ant waste is its poo. **B** and **C** are incorrect because ants don't have garbage and they don't have unwanted seeds.
6. You can judge that farmers grow food for themselves and others to eat. Ants take seeds to their nests and, when the seeds sprout, they can eat the shoots. Growing seeds in their nests for food makes ants like farmers.

Unit 13B PAGE 47

1. tunnels
2. larvae
3. spread
4. People
5. Suggested answers: grows, grown, growing, growth, grew
6. **A.**
7. larvae
8. endangered
9. C.
10. useful
11. **D.**
12. into the soil
13. C.
14. Let's make sure ants can do their jobs.
15. We don't want termites, ticks, flies and cockroaches in our homes.

ANSWERS

Unit 13C PAGE 48

1. **B.**
2. **A.**
3. **C.**
4. **A** and **B.**
5. **B.**
6. **B, C** and **D.**
7. Responses will vary.

Unit 14A PAGE 49

1. **A.** See line 10.
2. play, explore, climb, laugh (See lines 7–8.)
3. Responses will vary. Suggested answer: If someone is saying nasty things about you, your friend will stick up for you by telling them to stop.
4. **A.**
5. **C.**
6. Responses will vary. You can judge, for example, that a friend might tell you if you are being too bossy.

Unit 14B PAGE 50

1. troubles
2. truth
3. hurt
4. face
5. Suggested answers: celebrates, celebrated, celebrating, celebration, celebratory
6. **D.**
7. celebrate
8. disagree
9. **D.**
10. good
11. **D.**
12. by your side
13. **A.**
14. We're good friends.
15. It's good to have friends.

Unit 14C PAGE 51

1. **C.**
2. **D.**
3. care, share
4. To have your back means to be loyal, to protect you and to defend you against others.
5. Responses will vary. Suggested answers: celebrations such as birthdays, adventures, sporting events, outings, games
6. Responses will vary. Suggested answers: difficulties at home or at school, problems such as bullying, sadness over the loss of a pet
7. Responses will vary.

Unit 15A PAGE 52

1. **B.** See line 6.
2. **C.** See lines 7–10 and 13–14.
3. **C.**
4. **B.**
5. **A** and **B.** You can work out that **A** is true because the text states Linda has made many friends through tennis. You can work out that **B** is true because Ingrid is Linda's niece and she plays tennis. You can work out that **C** is not true because Linda's husband is a tennis coach and so would be able to play tennis.
6. You can judge that the text is all about how important tennis is to Linda.

Unit 15B PAGE 53

1. Uncle
2. Aunty
3. accident
4. rule
5. Suggested answers: disability, disabled, ability, inability
6. **B.**
7. traditional
8. volunteer coach
9. **A.**
10. traditional
11. **C.**
12. at their local club/at the tennis club
13. **D.** (**A** is also acceptable.)
14. Linda and Connor can't stop smiling.
15. Some players have hip, leg, spine or foot disabilities.

Unit 15C PAGE 54

1. **A.**
2. **B.**
3. **C.**
4. **B.**
5. **B, E** and **F.**
6. Responses will vary. Ingrid seems impressed by the positive impact tennis has had on Linda's life. Tennis gives Linda a happy life. It keeps her fit and she can make new friends.
7. Responses will vary.

NAPLAN-style Reading Test 2 PAGE 55

1. Be fantastic—don't use plastic. (See line 12.)
2. **D.** See lines 2–3.
3. **B.**
4. **B, C** and **D.** You can work out that people litter and the wind blows plastic and other litter into rivers that end up in the ocean. Rain also washes the plastic into the gutters and from there it goes into rivers and/or out to sea. People on boats and ships litter too.
5. **D.**
6. **A, B, C** and **D.** The text mentions the harm caused to people and animals. You can judge that plastic also harms the oceans and rivers. It

pollutes them. Plastic breaks down into smaller and smaller pieces.

7. **A** and **B**. Readers should feel angry that a careless person has dropped that plastic and it's ended up in the waterway. People should feel sad that the swan is trying to eat plastic.

NAPLAN-style Conventions of Language Test 2 — PAGE 56

1. Principal
2. everywhere
3. packaged
4. excited
5. competition
6. **B**.
7. **C**.
8. **D**.
9. **C**.
10. black swan, excited children, dead whale, reusable container
11. **C**.
12. **D**.
13. **C**.
14. **C**.

Unit 16A — PAGE 57

1. **A**. See lines 2–3.
2. soup with noodles (See line 7.)
3. band, sister
4. **B**.
5. No
6. You can judge that Ryan liked the food best because it's the first thing he mentions in paragraph one. Paragraph two is about the food. Paragraph three begins with 'The band was good too.'

Unit 16B — PAGE 58

1. different
2. music
3. bottles
4. phone
5. Suggested answers: compost, composted, composting
6. **B**.
7. compostable
8. stalls
9. **A**.
10. **A**.
11. liked
12. energetically
13. **A**.
14. 'Thanks for taking us,' said Ryan.
15. 'I had fun,' said Mum.

Unit 16C — PAGE 59

1. **B**.
2. **C**.
3. 1 **B**. 2 **D**. 3 **E**. 4 **C**. 5 **A**.
4. Chinese san choy bow; Mexican tacos; Japanese sushi; Italian pasta; Greek moussaka
5. **A**.
6. Responses will vary. You would most likely say you would enjoy the event for the same reasons Ryan enjoyed it: because of the food and the music.
7. Responses will vary.

Unit 17A — PAGE 60

1. on board a pirate ship (See line 3.)
2. **C**. See lines 3 and 8–9.
3. You can work out that they fought for it and stole it.
4. You can infer that they will keep it to eat.
5. **A**.
6. Responses will vary. You can judge from the text that the life of the characters sounds exciting, difficult and dangerous.

Unit 17B — PAGE 61

1. treasure
2. Burying
3. We'll
4. remember
5. Suggested answers: shared, sharing, shares
6. **C**.
7. port
8. coins
9. **C**.
10. **B**.
11. e.g. said, advised, praised
12. bravely
13. **D**. (**C** is also acceptable.)
14. 'We should bury it,' said Anne.
15. 'I agree,' said Mary.

Unit 17C — PAGE 62

1. **B**.
2. **B**.
3. the goods that were stolen: Spanish gold coins, rubies, diamonds, rice, sugar and bolts of cloth
4. **B**.
5. **D**.
6. **A**.
7. Responses will vary.

Unit 18A — PAGE 63

1. Gold Coast City Council (See line 25.)
2. Karaoke (See line 15.)
3. Cycling circuits, skate and scooter sessions
4. You can infer that this activity involves learning magic tricks and learning how to be a magician.
5. Nature spy and pottery require booking. The text states that they have limited places available.

6. You should judge that the photo shows a flying fox. It is likely part of an obstacle course or part of the Ninja warrior activity.

Unit 18B PAGE 64

1. program
2. obstacle
3. equipment
4. challenges
5. Suggested answers: avail, availability, unavailability
6. **B**.
7. karaoke
8. Fees
9. **D**.
10. **A**.
11. are
12. promptly
13. **C**.
14. The program begins on 21 August.
15. Have a look at the Gold Coast City Council website.

Unit 18C PAGE 65

1. **A**.
2. **A**.
3. **A**, **B**, **C**, **D** and **E**.
4. 4 (lines 3, 4, 6 and 18)
5. Responses will vary according to your interests but could include drama, art, craft, science experiments, environmental awareness, tennis, horse riding and swimming.
6. Responses will vary although you should judge that the poster is likely to be effective in encouraging children to join the program. The activities are varied, mostly free and sound like fun.
7. Responses will vary.

Unit 19A PAGE 66

1. the Royal National Park (See line 13.)
2. red (See line 6.)
3. **C**.
4. tall eucalypts and casuarina trees, cabbage-tree palms, Gymea lilies
5. different birds and the water trickling in the creek
6. You can judge that Dad would be pleased and proud of his daughter's knowledge of the National Park's trees and plants, and the fact that her favourite place is a place he takes her to.

Unit 19B PAGE 67

1. cabbages
2. peaceful
3. kilometres
4. world
5. Suggested answers: supply, supplied, supplying
6. **B**.
7. National Park/rainforest
8. quite
9. **D**.
10. **A**.
11. grow
12. leisurely
13. **C** or **D**.
14. We go hiking in the Royal National Park.
15. Dad, Roshni and Tami have lunch at Bola Creek.

Unit 19C PAGE 68

1. **A**.
2. **B**.
3. 1 **C**. 2 **A**. 3 **D**. 4 **B**.
4. eucalypts, casuarina trees, cabbage tree palms, Gymea lilies
5. The picnic spot is close in distance to the city but Tami cannot hear any traffic or city noise. She can only see nature and hear birds and the creek so it seems like the city is not close by at all.
6. Responses will vary.
7. Responses will vary.

Unit 20A PAGE 69

1. **B** and **E**. See lines 5–7.
2. **A**, **B**, **C**, **D** and **F**. See lines 8–14.
3. **B**. You can work out that stage fright is being frightened about being on stage and performing for an audience.
4. You can work out that playing in a band helps you overcome anxiety about performing in front of an audience because you are not alone. You have a team of band members to support you.
5. You can work out that being a member of a band helps you learn about being a member of a team. All band members need to practise and be reliable and responsible. They respect, support and encourage each other.
6. Responses will vary.

Unit 20B PAGE 70

1. assembly
2. musical
3. achievement
4. language
5. Suggested answers: chose, chosen, choice, choosing
6. **C**.
7. percussion
8. experience
9. **C**.
10. **B**.

ANSWERS

11. is
12. steadily
13. **B.**
14. We meet Tuesdays and Thursdays.
15. Choose from clarinet, euphonium, flute, percussion, saxophone, trombone or trumpet.

Unit 20C PAGE 71

1. **B.**
2. **C.**
3. **A**, **B** and **D.**
4. Responses will vary.
5. **B** and **C.**
6. The photos show that the band is inclusive of all children. For example, the photos show a boy, some girls and a child with a disability.
7. Responses will vary.

Unit 21A PAGE 72

1. soccer (See line 2.)
2. **A.** See line 12.
3. **B.** You can work out that, while it's nice to win and it's important to thank the other team, the best thing is having fun.
4. **C.** You can work out that a good sport is gracious in defeat as well as victory. You need to lose well and not be a sore loser.
5. **A.** You can work out that a coach teaches you how to play, how to be a team member and how to be a good winner and a good loser. Without a coach there would likely not be a team.
6. trying our hardest and always doing our best

Unit 21B PAGE 73

1. individual
2. competitions
3. disappointing
4. Congratulate
5. Suggested answers: coaches, coaching, coached
6. **B.**
7. blame
8. sport
9. **A.**
10. **B.**
11. remember
12. quickly
13. **A.**
14. 'I don't like team sport,' said Simon.
15. 'Ms Chen is our soccer coach,' said Tara.

Unit 21C PAGE 74

1. **B.**
2. **B.**
3. **C.**
4. Tara speaks for herself (I) and her team (we), whereas Simon only speaks for himself (I) because he is not a member of a team.
5. You should judge that each child has clearly presented opinions and reasoning. It is easy to understand their points of view.
6. Responses will vary. You might say that Tara's opinion is closer to your own because you enjoy team sports. Or you may decide that Simon's attitude to sport is closer to your own because you prefer individual sports.
7. Responses will vary.

Unit 22A PAGE 75

1. breathing out and making it in cars and factories (See lines 7–8.)
2. oxygen (See line 6.)
3. **A**, **B** and **C.**
4. Soil could blow away in the wind or wash away in the rain.
5. You can work out that, most importantly, trees make oxygen that all animals, including humans, must breathe to survive.
6. Responses will vary.

Unit 22B PAGE 76

1. beautiful
2. possible
3. carbon
4. Possums
5. Suggested answers: shady, shades, shaded, shading
6. **B.**
7. buffer
8. oxygen
9. **D.**
10. **B.**
11. am
12. sincerely
13. **D.**
14. 'Thank you for being here,' said Josef.
15. 'I love trees,' said Chanel.

Unit 22C PAGE 77

1. **B.**
2. **A.** You can work out that the text is for children because of the way it is written and the photo of the child that is included.
3. 1 **B.** 2 **C.** 3 **D.** 4 **E.** 5 **A.**
4. **B.**
5. Responses will vary. You might say the text made no difference to how you feel about trees

because you already value and love trees. Or you may feel that the text made you realise just how important trees are.

6. Responses will vary. You could suggest that people plant more trees or that we should protect trees and forests from being cut down.
7. Responses will vary.

Unit 23A PAGE 78

1. Bundaberg (See line 2.)
2. in her bathroom (See lines 3–4.)
3. **A**, **B** and **C**.
4. You can work out that the wind twists. It moves in a spiral.
5. **A**, **B** and **C**.
6. Responses will vary. You can judge that when you are terrified, the thing that frightens you seems to last for ages. Time seems to go more slowly.

Unit 23B PAGE 79

1. Tornadoes
2. column
3. Emergency
4. survived
5. Suggested answers: terrify, terrified, terrifies
6. **B**.
7. deafening
8. thunderstorm
9. **D**.
10. a powerful column of wind OR a powerful column of wind from a thunderstorm
11. will
12. fearfully
13. **A**.
14. 'We were terrified,' declared Zara.
15. 'How is your house?' asked Chris.

Unit 23C PAGE 80

1. **C**.
2. **C**.
3. **A**, **B**, **C** and **D**.
4. crashing, banging, terrifying, deafening, survived
5. Responses will vary.
6. Responses will vary. Note that news reports aim to interest readers and viewers. They use emotive language and photos to bring newsworthy events to their audiences. A news report needs to be interesting enough to hold viewers' attention. Audiences stop viewing if the news does not interest them.
7. Responses will vary.

NAPLAN-style Reading Test 3 PAGE 81

1. **B**. See lines 11–12.
2. spinach, fetta cheese (See lines 6–7.)
3. **C**.
4. **A**, **C** and **D**.
5. **A**.
6. **A**, **B** and **C**. **A** is correct because Yia Yia is a good cook so the cake will taste good. **B** is also a correct answer because family members will want to eat the cake Yia Yia baked. **D** is incorrect. The fact that the cake is served at family gatherings is not a reason for wanting a piece.
7. **A**, **B**, **D**, **E** and **F**.

NAPLAN-style Conventions of Language Test 3 PAGE 82

1. does
2. planning
3. especially
4. youngest
5. loving
6. **C**.
7. **D**.
8. **B**.
9. **C**.
10. **C**.
11. **A**.
12. **C**.
13. **C**.
14. **B**.

Unit 24A PAGE 83

1. Brisbane (See lines 13 and 22.)
2. **B**. See lines 12 and 21.
3. The $120 tent. The text says it is ultra-lightweight.
4. The $79 tent. The text says it's strong and has a heavy-duty floor.
5. The $120 tent. The text says it is an automatic pop-up tent.
6. Responses will vary but you should judge that the most important features are that it's waterproof and easy to put up. Other good features include that it is lightweight. Zip openings and storage panels are great features but not as important as waterproofing.

Unit 24B PAGE 84

1. Heavy-duty
2. private
3. waterproof
4. lightweight
5. Suggested answers: store, stores, stored, storing
6. **B**.
7. automatic
8. storage
9. **C**.
10. velcro storm flaps
11. has been used/was used
12. out
13. so
14. Contact Pratika in Brisbane to buy the $79 tent.

ANSWERS

15. 'I prefer the orange tent,' said Elizabeth.

Unit 24C PAGE 85

1. **B**.
2. **C**.
3. **A**, **B** and **C**.
4. Responses will vary. Most likely you will say that the photo of the $79 tent shows you the size of the tent better because someone is lying in the tent. It's hard to judge the size of the $120 tent. Both tents are advertised as two-person tents but the $79 tent seems larger due to the photo provided.
5. **A**. You can work out that **B** and **C** are incorrect because the tents are advertised as almost new and as new.
6. Responses will vary. You would choose the tent that suits your lifestyle. If you hike and need to carry your tent in a backpack, you will choose the lightest. If weight is not an issue you will choose the one that seems the most comfortable or largest. If cost is important you might choose the cheapest one.
7. Responses will vary.

Unit 25A PAGE 86

1. **B**. See line 3.
2. **B**, **C** and **D**. See lines 16–17.
3. **A**.
4. **A**, **B** and **C**.
5. **A**. You can work out that they are breaking the law and should be punished, i.e. fined or jailed.
6. You can judge that an aquarium is not a happy place for a large animal that usually swims long distances in the open sea. The whale shark would feel sad, bored and probably lonely. It would feel trapped and frightened.

Unit 25B PAGE 87

1. ocean
2. whale
3. International
4. plankton
5. Suggested answers: hunt, hunts, hunting, hunter
6. **B**.
7. hunted
8. filter
9. **B**.
10. a school bus
11. are not
12. during migration
13. Although
14. Some are kept in aquariums in Japan, the USA and China.
15. 'I feel sad for whale sharks in fish tanks,' said Jed.

Unit 25C PAGE 88

1. **A**.
2. **B**.
3. **A** false **B** true **C** true **D** false **E** true **F** false
4. **A**, **B**, **C** and **F**.
5. **C**.
6. **B**.
7. Responses will vary.

Unit 26A PAGE 89

1. **B**. See line 2.
2. **C**, **D** and **F**. See lines 2–3.
3. **C**.
4. **B**. You can work out that webbed feet help an animal to swim but are not much use for digging or for walking on land.
5. **B**.
6. You can judge that land clearing is the biggest threat because it destroys platypus habitats. Yabby traps and lack of food also kill platypuses but land clearing kills them on a large scale.

Unit 26B PAGE 90

1. platypus
2. Males
3. venomous
4. caught
5. Suggested answers: covers, covered, covering, uncovered, recovered
6. **A**.
7. venomous
8. nostrils
9. **B**.
10. back feet and tail
11. are being destroyed
12. along the east coast of Australia
13. because
14. It scoops insects, worms, mud, small rocks, shellfish and larvae into its bill.
15. 'It's quite cute,' said Pippa.

Unit 26C PAGE 91

1. **C**.
2. **B**.
3. 1 **C**. 2 **D**. 3 **B**. 4 **A**.
4. Responses will vary. Suggested answers: **A** duck **B** duck **C** dog **D** bird **E** wombat
5. **A**. You can work out that **B** cannot be true because males would want to attract females and not fight them off. **C** cannot be true because of the type of food a platypus eats (See line 6.). The platypus does not need toxic spurs to kill these types of creatures.
6. You can judge that saving and preserving creeks and rivers will save the habitat that the platypus needs so that it does not become extinct.
7. Responses will vary.

ANSWERS

Unit 27A PAGE 92

1. tea-tree (See lines 4–5.)
2. Gumbi Gumbi and Umbrella bush wattle (See lines 7–9.)
3. **A**, **C**, **D**, **E** and **F**.
4. **A** and **D**. You can work out that something used for cuts and sores would be applied to skin. **E** could also be correct as many treatments for joint pain are applied to the skin.
5. **B**, **C**, **E** and **F**. You can work out that fruit, tea and cough mixture can be swallowed.
6. Responses will vary.

Unit 27B PAGE 93

1. medicine
2. antiseptic
3. throat
4. relief
5. Suggested answers: stronger, strongest, strength, strengthen, strengthened
6. **A**.
7. antiseptic
8. medicines
9. **D**.
10. Australian native lemongrass leaves, stems and roots
11. soaked; boiled
12. For thousands of years
13. but
14. Leaves, stems and roots are used to make tea.
15. 'First Nations Australians use bush medicine,' said Ethan.

Unit 27C PAGE 94

1. **C**.
2. **C**.
3. **B**.
4. **C**.
5. **A**, **B**, **C**, **D** and **F**.
6. Responses will vary. They are excited because they are only just discovering the benefits of bush medicine and there must be so much more to find out about them.
7. Responses will vary.

Unit 28A PAGE 95

1. 1829 (See line 2.)
2. **A** and **B**. See lines 7, 10 and 17.
3. **A**, **B**, **C** and **D**. You can work out that the spider is all of these things. The spider is a tricky character who tells lies and tries to charm victims into believing the lies.
4. **A** and **D**. You can work out that the fly has heard about the spider's ways and will be too clever and strong-willed to get caught in the spider's trap.
5. **A**, **C** and **F**. You can work out that the spider is trying to charm the fly so the voice will be sweet, smooth and kindly. The spider would not use a loud, harsh or angry voice as this would frighten the fly away.
6. You can judge that the spider is trying to trap the fly in order to eat it. The offers are not real or genuine. The spider is not being kind or generous. The spider is being tricky and devious.

Unit 28B PAGE 96

1. prettiest
2. soaring
3. winding
4. heard
5. Suggested answers: sleep, sleeper, sleeping, slept, asleep, sleepy, sleepily, sleepless, sleeplessness
6. **D**.
7. fine
8. drawn
9. **C**.
10. my little bed
11. caught
12. up a winding stair
13. and
14. 'Will you come into my parlour?' asked a spider.
15. 'I have a cosy bed for a fly,' declared the spider.

Unit 28C PAGE 97

1. **A**.
2. **B**.
3. The illustration shows a cartoon spider. This spider suits a fiction text. A photo would show a real spider. A photo would suit a factual text.
4. **A**.
5. **A**.
6. **B**.
7. Responses will vary.

Unit 29A PAGE 98

1. drones, gyrocopters, electronic devices (See lines 13–14.)
2. every species/sharks (See lines 15–16.)
3. because she is a shark expert/ to ask her opinion about shark nets
4. **C**.
5. **B**. All three answers are true but the Professor is most concerned that nets kill harmless animals including whales, dolphins and turtles, as well as harmless sharks.
6. You can judge that Professor Hamden is opposed to shark nets. It would also be useful to hear from an expect who supports shark nets. This would give balance to the topic.

Unit 29B PAGE 99

1. unnecessarily
2. essential
3. endangered
4. technology
5. Suggested answers: enclosed, enclosing, enclosure, encloses
6. **B**.
7. repel
8. unnecessarily
9. **A**.
10. Very few people
11. can be used
12. in nets
13. but
14. 'Many harmless animals get tangled and die,' said Sofia.
15. 'What do you think about netting?' asked Philip.

Unit 29C PAGE 100

1. **A**.
2. **B**.
3. **B**.
4. whales, turtles and dolphins
5. Most sharks are harmless. Only some sharks will bite people and not many people get bitten by sharks.
6. Responses will vary.
7. Responses will vary.

Unit 30A PAGE 101

1. **B**. See lines 5–6.
2. on three islands off the coast of Tasmania (See lines 3–4.)
3. **A** and **C**. Note that **B** is incorrect because the text states that the birds are adding to the concrete nests to improve them. They are not lazy. They just can't find enough vegetation to make their own nests.
4. They drown.
5. **C**, **D** and **E**.
6. You can judge that people are the cause of climate change and so people are to blame for the albatross's problems.

Unit 30B PAGE 102

1. Conservationists
2. surviving
3. vegetation
4. difficult
5. Suggested answers: returns, returned, returning
6. **D**.
7. chicks
8. protection
9. **B**.
10. Scientists, conservationists and park rangers
11. added
12. on islands off Tasmania/each year
13. Because
14. 'They breed on Albatross Island,' said Lexi.
15. 'Do they like their new nests?' asked Louis.

Unit 30C PAGE 103

1. **B**.
2. **A**.
3. 1 **C**. 2 **B**. 3 **A**.
4. **A**, **B** and **D**. You can work out that these are the specific groups concerned about the albatrosses and their nests.
5. They spend their time travelling.
6. You might find this very sad or it could make you angry. Shy albatrosses nearly became extinct because people wanted their feathers to make hats. (In around 1870 dead, stuffed birds were mounted on the hats, not just feathers.) Some birds became extinct because they were killed for their feathers. The passenger pigeon is an example. Feathers are still used in the hat industry today. When parent birds are killed, their chicks are left to die because they have no-one to feed them or care for them.
7. Responses will vary.

NAPLAN-style Reading Test 4 PAGE 104

1. **A** and **B**. See lines 12–13.
2. **A**, **B** and **C**. See lines 7–8.
3. **A**, **B** and **C**.
4. Responses will vary. You should infer that most non-Aboriginal people did not like the Aboriginal children speaking languages they did not understand. Many non-Aboriginal people did not value or respect Aboriginal culture, language or tradition.
5. **A** and **B**.
6. **B** and **C**.
7. **A**, **B**, **C** and **E**.

NAPLAN-style Conventions of Language Test 4 PAGE 105

1. Aboriginal
2. families
3. traditional
4. generations
5. suffered
6. **C**.
7. **C**.
8. **D**.
9. **C**.
10. **C**.
11. **D**.
12. **B**.
13. **D**.
14. **B**.

ANSWERS

Updated in 2025 for the NSW Curriculum and Australian Curriculum Version 9.0 changes

ISBN 978 1 74125 648 2

Pascal Press
PO Box 250
Glebe NSW 2037
(02) 9198 1748
www.pascalpress.com.au

Publisher: Vivienne Joannou
Project editor: Mark Dixon
Edited and proofread by Mark Dixon
Answers checked by Dale Little
Cover and page design by Sonia Woo
Typeset by Grizzly Graphics (Leanne Richters)
Printed by Vivar Printing/Green Giant Press